THE
COLLEGE
BUCKET
LIST

THE COLLEGE BUCKET LIST

101
**Fun, Unforgettable,
and *Maybe Even* Life-Changing
Things to Do Before Graduation Day**

Kourtney Jason
Darcy Pedersen

Ulysses Press

Text copyright © 2016 Kourtney Jason and Darcy Pedersen. Concept and design
copyright © 2016 Ulysses Press and its licensors. All rights reserved. Any
unauthorized duplication in whole or in part or dissemination of this edition by
any means (including but not limited to photocopying, electronic devices, digital
versions, and the Internet) will be prosecuted to the fullest extent of the law.

Published in the United States by:
Ulysses Press
P.O. Box 3440
Berkeley, CA 94703
www.ulyssespress.com

ISBN13: 978-1-61243-642-5
Library of Congress Control Number: 2016950670

Printed in the United States by United Graphics Inc.

10 9 8 7 6 5 4 3 2 1

Acquisitions editor: Casie Vogel
Managing editor: Claire Chun
Project editor: Caety Klingman
Editor: Renee Rutledge
Proofreader: Shayna Keyles
Front cover and interior design: what!design @ whatweb.com
Cover artwork: photo © Rawpixel.com/shutterstock.com
Interior artwork: banner on pages 3, 25, 65, 79, 139, 169, 195, 219
    © jekson_js/shutterstock.com; icons on pages 25, 65, 79, 139, 169, 195,
    219 © ekler/shutterstock.com; icon on page 3 © andromina/shutterstock.com

Distributed by Publishers Group West

CONTENTS

THINGS THAT ARE GOOD FOR YOUR HEALTH 125

INTRODUCTION

Hey there, undergrad! It's good to see you. We are so excited you've picked up *The College Bucket List*.

Whether you bought this book yourself or received it as a gift, you are in for an exciting ride. That's coming from two women with college degrees from a certified party school, so you know we know how to have a good time. And we're here to spill all we learned as coeds.

Within these pages are 101 secrets, tried-and-true tips, life lessons, and unforgettable activities to make your time in college the best years of your life. This bucket list covers the gamut from your first day on campus through graduation day, when you don that cap and gown. You'll find everything from rites of passage and things to share on Instagram and Snapchat to things NOT to tell mom or grandma (the horror!) and ways to ignite your school spirit (rah rah siss boom ba!).

Each bucket list item comes complete with our reasoning as to why it made the list as well as advice and tips on how and when to accomplish it. Within the span of four (or five) years, each and every college student can find the time to complete *The College Bucket List*. With this book, you'll make incredible memories and graduate without regrets.

THINGS THAT WILL IGNITE YOUR SCHOOL SPIRIT

After touring a couple universities and crushing the admissions tests, you've finally received that acceptance letter in the mail. It is an exciting moment, isn't it? As soon as you respond with your intention to enroll, you officially become a Lion, Bear, Wildcat, or (insert your school mascot here)! On the following pages, you'll find all the bucket list items—from starting your collection of college apparel to joining in on a long-lasting school tradition—that will make you proud to represent your university.

■

EXPLORE YOUR CAMPUS

Question: How much do you really know about your college campus? Sure, you can find the student center and cafeteria, and you probably have a pretty good idea of your way around most of the buildings. But, odds are, there are a lot more places to explore and history to know about your campus than you previously thought. A definite college must is to get to know your turf, inside and out.

One of the easiest ways to start is to take a campus tour. Maybe you got a basic tour your freshman year, but if there is a more in-depth tour that focuses on the history of your school, be sure and take it at least once. You'll be amazed at what you learn.

Another, more adventurous way to get to know your campus? Explore all the hidden nooks and crannies in a stealthier fashion! Every building undoubtedly has a basement, little-used rooms, and even a roof that's just begging to be explored. For safety reasons, it's best to bring along a friend or two for this excursion to serve as a lookout or help you get out of a tight spot. Not a whole group, though (you don't want to bring any unwanted attention to yourselves). Befriend one of the maintenance/janitorial workers and see if they have any tidbits to any particularly cool parts of campus to explore. Or they could even leave a door unlocked sometime, cough cough.

As always, practice common sense (no getting drunk on the roof!), and above all, do not get caught! Be careful exploring the campus after hours (silent alarms and video cameras will no doubt be plentiful). If caught, plead ignorance. Pretend you got lost, apologize, and GTFO stat! Lastly, if the situation seems too risky, just don't do it. You don't want to do anything that would jeopardize your enrollment. Try explaining that to your parents!

VOLUNTEER AT THE CAMPUS RADIO STATION

Do you regularly impress people with the depth of your musical knowledge? Is music a constant part of your life? Do you make a beeline to the jukebox whenever you enter a bar? Then why not consider volunteering at the campus radio station?!

Think about it: a block of airtime for you to play whatever your heart desires! So how do you make your time slot stand out from the rest of the station formats and the other bland radio stations playing the same top 40 songs? Think of devoting your time to a theme, like a form of music not usually heard on mainstream radio (Broadway songs, Bollywood music, old school hip hop, to name a few). Advertise your station and get regular listeners, then consider opening a request line to keep them engaged. Oh, and a clever DJ name is a must, of course.

Another bonus: this will be another extracurricular activity that will look great on a resume.

Did You Know? World College Radio Day is November 4!

SPEND A SPRING OR WINTER BREAK ON CAMPUS

There are many reasons why you could end up not going home for a school break. Maybe you're low on funds and would rather save your money. Or you have a ton of schoolwork you want to catch up on, or have an off-campus job that won't give you the time off. Or maybe you just want to spend some quality time in your college town without the added hassle of actually having to go to class. Whatever the reason, staying on campus during a break is something you should try at least once to make the most of your college experience. Let us count the ways:

1. Whether you live in the dorms or at an apartment/house with roommates, odds are you will have the place to yourself. How often does that happen? We're guessing never! Take full advantage of that freedom and binge-watch some TV, experiment with cooking in the kitchen, blast the music you like, and dance around in your underwear—the possibilities are endless.

2. If you have a job, see if you can take some extra shifts and make some extra beer money for the rest of the semester! If you don't have one, pick up a side gig or two for some extra cash (see page 192).

3. Use it as an opportunity to meet new friends! Look around and see who else decided to stay home for break.

4. Even the most popular bars, restaurants, and coffee shops will be gloriously uncrowded. Go out and get served immediately.

5. Fallen behind in any of your classes? Want to get a head start on a big project? Now is the perfect time for some uninterrupted, hardcore studying with no distractions.

6. You know what else is uncrowded during this time? The gym! Get a head start on your fitness and relish not having to wait your turn for the elliptical.

These are just some of the reasons that sticking around your school during a break can sometimes be more relaxing, fun, and productive than going home. Give it a try at least once, you might love it!

BUY SCHOOL SWAG

Check this off your bucket list right before you graduate. Buy everything and anything with "Alumni" on it! You deserve it—you're graduating!

If you are just starting at your school, you'll definitely want to get some swag to wear around campus and to events.

During orientation, you can pick up a shirt or a sweatshirt. And you'll likely be able to get your parents to pay for it (win!). They may even pick up something for themselves with your school's name and "Mom" or "Dad" on it, or maybe a bumper sticker for their car. Typical.

Once you start your first semester, you may also want to pick up a pennant to hang up in your room.

Other school swag you'll want to check out? They've got everything at your school's bookstore! T-shirts and tanks, sweatshirts, outerwear, shorts and pants, accessories, polo shirts, hats, sweaters and woven shirts, dresses, and more. With plenty of designs, styles, and colors, you'll find school swag you must have. Sometimes it's a little pricey, so make sure not to go overboard and only pick out the pieces you know you will wear. Sweatshirts are a popular purchase, and they have the most variety in terms of designs available.

You can wear your school attire anywhere, on campus and off. If you like to attend campus events, it's great to wear the school colors to show off your school pride.

LEARN YOUR COLLEGE FIGHT SONG

Every school has a college fight song. And these songs can date back to the earliest years of the school's establishment. Yale's "Boola Boola" fight song dates back to 1900. "Come Join the Band," Stanford's fight song, was written in 1907. "Big C," the fight song of UC Berkeley, was composed in 1913. These songs are ancient! So, in total hipster fashion, it's time to bring these ditties back into the limelight.

Those in the most recent generations don't know their school fight songs, unless you're in the marching band and you're required to know it.

It is probably easy enough to find the lyrics with a quick Google search. Print them out and pass the lyrics out to your group of friends. There should also be a recording online somewhere so you can learn the tempo. Study the lyrics and memorize them with your friends. Then, the next time you're at a big game and the marching band plays the song, you can all sing along. You may even inspire the groups next to you to learn the songs before the next big game.

If you're watching a big away game at a bar, start the sing-along then. Come prepared with lyric sheets for other bar patrons so they can join in on your fun!

PARTICIPATE IN SCHOOL TRADITIONS

Every school has some sort of wacky tradition that has been going on for ages. Sometimes it's hard to even know how these traditions got started, or they've spun so far off from the original event that it's hilarious. No matter what traditions your school offers, it's always fun to participate and feel like you belong.

Here, we've rounded up some of the most interesting, fun, and straight up weird college traditions.

1. **ORGO NIGHT (COLUMBIA UNIVERSITY):** Organic chemistry is one of the most intense and rigorous classes offered at Columbia. So to help organic chem students take a break while cramming for their final, the Columbia marching bands head to the library for a mini concert complete with the fight song, jokes, and music.

2. **SHOE TREE (MURRAY STATE UNIVERSITY):** Just outside the library, a large tree has been covered with mismatched shoes. Couples who meet while attending MSU nail their shoes (one from each person) to the tree, but no one knows how long this

has been happening. It is said that by hanging their shoes, they'll have a happy life together. Some alumni have returned to hang a baby shoe after they have kids. And if you happen to break up? Maybe if you really liked that shoe, you could go get it back.

3. **RUB THE TOE (YALE UNIVERSITY):** Theodore Dwight Woolsey, class of 1820 and former president of Yale University, has a commemorative statue on campus. It is common lore that if you rub the toe of Woolsey's shoes, some of his luck will rub off on you.

4. **SERENADES (VASSAR COLLEGE):** The day originated with each class serenading the seniors with class songs and original pieces. These days, the freshmen compose original songs (that aren't always too kind) for the seniors. In retaliation, the seniors get to attack the freshman with water balloons and Super Soakers.

5. **TOAST TOSS (UNIVERSITY OF PENNSYLVANIA):** Students toss pieces of toast onto the field after the third quarter of home football games. The school even has a Zamboni to clean up the bread.

6. **PUMPKIN DROP (MUIR COLLEGE):** Students watch an oversized pumpkin (stuffed with candy!) drop from the eleventh story of Tioga Hall.

7. **DOOLEY'S WEEK (EMORY UNIVERSITY):** Dooley, the school's unofficial mascot, drops by various classes unannounced to let students out for the day.

8. **SPREE DAY (CLARK UNIVERSITY):** School administrators spontaneously cancel classes and host a celebration filled with bands and entertainment for students.

9. **SKI-BEACH DAY (POMONA UNIVERSITY):** Only in Southern California can you drive to snow-covered mountains and the beach on the same day. In February or March, a busload of students heads to Mountain High to hit the slopes. Then, by afternoon, they are back on the bus and heading toward Newport Beach for some fun in the sun.

7

TAILGATE BEFORE A COLLEGE SPORTING EVENT

To start the big game on the right note, one must tailgate. Nothing like pregaming in a parking lot to get your excitement building!

With a few essential ingredients and your pals by your side, tailgating is a tradition that lives on for a reason. If your school is known for having big sports teams, the tailgating might even be on another level. And it doesn't stop when you graduate college. Alumni regularly join in on the fun during homecoming, big rivalries, and championship games.

And tailgating expands beyond collegiate sports—you can tailgate before professional sports games or even before concerts.

To properly tailgate, you'll want to start about four hours before the game. That way, you'll have time to set up, clean up, and enjoy yourself in between.

Here is your checklist to make sure your tailgate is a success:

- ❏ Beer
- ❏ Ice
- ❏ Cooler
- ❏ Chairs
- ❏ Meat
- ❏ Grill
- ❏ Charcoal
- ❏ Lighter fluid
- ❏ Table
- ❏ Cheese
- ❏ Ketchup
- ❏ Buns
- ❏ Chips

- ❏ Spatula
- ❏ Plates
- ❏ Napkins
- ❏ Bluetooth speakers (to connect to your smartphone)
- ❏ Solo cups (This particular brand is a party staple thanks to the measuring lines inside the cups!)
- ❏ Canopy (might be a splurge, but well worth it!)
- ❏ Games (Ping-Pong balls for Beer Pong, Cornhole, Flip Cup)

GO TO A GAME FOR EVERY SCHOOL SPORTS TEAM

It may take all four years to successfully accomplish this one, but it will be pure fun every step of the way. Some sports might not have the most enthusiastic fans as spectators, so your presence will mean all the more to the athletes.

For each game, you should tailgate, paint your face, take a selfie with the school mascot (if present), celebrate the big win, and even invite your parents to come along.

What sports does this entail? All of them, for both men's and women's teams! Though not all schools will have teams for every sport, the majority of schools will have some sort of athletic department. We're talking football, baseball, basketball, track and field, soccer, golf, softball, volleyball, crew, fencing, ice hockey, lacrosse, sailing, squash, field hockey, tennis, swimming and diving, cross country, gymnastics, skiing, water polo, wrestling, rugby, and anything else not mentioned here. Make a list of your school teams, then start researching the when and where for games and meets.

Check off the sports as you go to their games:

❑ baseball

❑ basketball (men's)

❑ basketball (women's)

❑ bowling

❑ cross country (men's)

❑ cross country (women's)

❑ fencing

❑ field hockey

❑ football

❑ golf (men's)

❑ golf (women's)

❑ gymnastics (men's)

❑ gymnastics (women's)

❑ ice hockey (men's)

❑ ice hockey (women's)

❑ lacrosse (men's)

❑ lacrosse (women's)

❑ rifle

❑ rowing

❑ skiing

❑ soccer (men's)

❑ soccer (women's)

❑ softball

❑ swimming and diving (men's)

❑ swimming and diving (women's)

❑ tennis (men's)

❑ tennis (women's)

❑ track and field (men's)

❑ track and field (women's)

❑ volleyball (men's)

❑ volleyball (women's)

❑ water polo (men's)

❑ water polo (women's)

❑ wrestling

PARTICIPATE IN A CAMPUS FUNDRAISER

You can find a number of ways to participate in campus fundraisers, from donating blood to buying a cupcake for a good cause. As you walk through campus day in and day out, you will regularly see someone doing something for a cause. Depending on the causes you believe in, you may choose to ignore most of these fundraisers. But for every few that you ignore, you should also participate in one.

1. You are young and healthy, so donating blood shouldn't take too much time or effort. Plus, it usually includes a snack at the end to make sure you don't pass out.

2. If you see a bake sale, why not treat yourself to a cookie or a cupcake?

3. If you see a dunk tank, why not give it a shot? You've got a good arm on ya!

4. If you see a coin drive, why not pass along some of the pennies in your piggy bank?

5. If there's a movie night on campus, gather your friends to join you.

6. If there's a raffle, why not see if lady luck is on your side?

7. If there's a rummage sale, why not go through your closet and find some pieces to donate?

For every fundraiser you help, you remind yourself of the importance to do good in the world. Take that with you. There will be days in your future that you forget.

10

ENJOY ON-CAMPUS EVENTS

Who can say no to inexpensive entertainment? Even big celebrity names, comedians, and well-known bands hit the road to tour college campuses. And students typically get first dibs on tickets prior to the general public.

Other on-campus events you can attend could be put on by your fellow students. Your campus radio station may have live events, such as a battle of the bands featuring local groups. Clubs host events to help support their programs, so maybe you could check out a movie night or comedy show. Another club might sponsor a famous author to do a book talk and signing on campus. Or maybe an artist has donated their artwork to be displayed in the campus gallery.

If your school has a theater program, you can see great productions for a fraction of the real Broadway price. Heck, you may even be going to school with the next Lin-Manuel Miranda, and you wouldn't know unless you put your butt in one of the theater's seats!

In short, the culture and entertainment on and around your campus is alive and well. And all of these events are within your budget. You just might have to do a little extra research to see what's happening.

You can follow school calendars, sign up for event newsletters, or pick up the school newspaper to stay up to date on who is coming to your school and when they'll be there. Make sure to see when tickets go on sale as some on-campus events are known to sell out.

Don't miss out on the cheap fun!

THINGS TO SHARE ON SOCIAL MEDIA

This chapter's bucket list items are all worth sharing on social media so that you have a record of these adventures and excursions for the rest of your life. It's like a visual diary of your college years.

Many of these experiences will include your friends. However, you may also find you prefer to explore a museum or study abroad on your own, in which case, these could be moments where you reflect on who you were, who you are, and who you're becoming.

Each item also lists suggested hashtags when posting on apps like Instagram. Don't forget to tag your friends too, so you can all look back on these memories for years to come.

Now, we will preemptively apologize for sounding like a parent to remind you about the dark side of social media. While in college, you may want to reevaluate your current privacy settings. You'll also want to make a conscious decision as to the kinds of "partying" posts (i.e., if you are drinking underage) you want to share. This stuff really does stay with you as well as live on the Internet forever. Like, forever forever. Parental talk over.

II

GO ON AN EPIC ROAD TRIP

College is the perfect time to experience one of America's great pastimes: the epic road trip! Perhaps you've only ever been on a long car trip with your family. Well strap the hell in, because going on a road trip with just your friends is one of the best ways to say, "I'm an adult now, dammit!"

The first and most obvious logistic: the destination. Maybe you have friends to visit across the country, or there is a music festival calling your name. Whatever the reason, a general idea of where you want to go and what you want to see is the first step to planning a kick-ass good time.

The next logical step will be to pick your road trip companions. This is a decision not to be made lightly. Long hours in a car will try the patience of the most Zen-like person out there, so think hard about who you want to be riding shotgun with you. High maintenance friends who do not take disruptions in their routines well should be avoided. A road trip is bound to have unexpected detours and tense moments, and something will go wrong with the plans. If your friend flips their shit if their order is messed up at Starbucks, it may be a good idea to leave them behind. Ditto the friend with expensive tastes, who will insist on eating in a nice restaurant and stay in a three-star hotel every night. It's not an authentic road trip without at least a few nights in campgrounds or in the back of the car and having to make a dinner out of what you can find in the 7-Eleven at the last pit stop.

Another tip: At the beginning of the trip, have everyone put in a set amount of money in an envelope. This will be the budget for gas and lodging. Also, do not be a stereo hog! Music is the bedrock of a successful road trip, and even if everyone in the car has wildly different tastes in music, share the air time equally. You may even find a new band to like!

If all goes well, your epic road trip will be something you and your friends will remember for life. And if you manage not to murder your friend for playing that same Taylor Swift album for three hours, you will achieve sainthood!

SUGGESTED HASHTAGS

- Create a specific hashtag for your road trip by combining your names and the place where you are going
- The roads you're taking (i.e. #route69)
- #roadtrip
- #ontheroad
- #hittingtheroad

- #driving
- #playlists
- #sightseeing
- #america
- #herewego
- #singalong
- #scenicroute
- #roadtripselfie
- #foodstop
- #travel
- #car
- #sightoftheday

12

ORGANIZE A WEEKEND CAMPING TRIP

Sometimes you just need to get away from it all and recharge. But if spring or summer break is a distant dream, we have just the solution: a weekend camping trip!

If you made it to the end of the week and another night out to the bars or to another frat party sounds more tiresome than fun, that means it is time to head for the hills. Grab some friends, pack the car with supplies, food, and booze, and let nature heal your studied-out soul.

If you aren't normally the camping type, here are some ways to keep costs down. Shop for sales and scour thrift stores for supplies you need, like a tent, flashlights, a sleeping bag, and a camp stove. For some items, like one big tent to crash in, you can split the cost with friends. Get creative with household items and repurpose them for your camping needs.

Find a campground within a comfortable driving distance from your campus, preferably with a lake or river nearby.

Then, grab a couple friends that also need some nature time. You could even organize a big group of people and take over a few campsites near each other. Bonus: less people to tell you to keep it down during quiet hours! Be sure to bring plenty of food that can be cooked over an open campfire. If you want to go gourmet, have at it. But camping was made for hot dogs, chips, chili, and other treats that taste like a five-star meal after exploring all day. Bring some fun card games or a football or two for entertainment around the campfire. Above all, do not schedule anything like a 20-mile hike up a mountain (unless that's your thing, in which case you do you. We'll be at the campfire with a beer if you need us.). The point of a weekend break in nature is to unwind, bond with your friends, get silly, and come back to campus relaxed and ready for another week stuck in a classroom.

SUGGESTED HASHTAGS

- Create a hashtag for your camping trip by combining the location or campground with your group name
- #camping
- #campingtrip
- #campinglife
- #fire
- #tents
- #cookingonthefire
- #nature

- #livinginnature
- #sleepingunderthestars
- #cardgames
- #lakelife
- #riverlife
- #smores
- #countrylife
- #grillinandchillin

13

EXPLORE YOUR TOWN BEYOND THE CAMPUS NEIGHBORHOOD

A curious phenomena tends to happen around college campuses: with housing, school, bars, and stores all clustered around one central area, it can begin to feel like the only people on the planet are people your age (minus the professors). Time to see what else this town has to offer! Go outside the perimeter of the school and the college "bubble" to find interesting ethnic neighborhoods, new bars and restaurants, and people of all different ages. Even if the outer area is bland suburbs and big box stores, it still makes for an enlightening experience that will remind you there is another world out there beyond classes and homework.

OUTSIDE-THE-COMFORT-ZONE IDEAS

1. Go to a non-college bar and chat up some locals. Hit on a townie!

2. Have a picnic in a park full of families.

3. See live music in a venue that caters to an older crowd, like a jazz club.

4. Visit a local landmark.

5. Try a new restaurant. Expand your culinary horizons with Greek, Thai, vegan, raw oysters—anything you've never tried before!

6. Go to your town's library instead of the one on campus.

7. Don't just see the plays put on by your school's theater department. Catch a show at a local theater company.

8. Learn your town's history by going on a walking tour or sightseeing bus. See your town from a tourist's perspective!

So be sure and make a weekend out of seeing what your town or city has to offer besides the college. Not only will it expand your mind, but you just might fall in love with the non-college parts of your town!

SUGGESTED HASHTAGS

- The Zip Code or Area Code

- Your City

- Your State

- #visit + your city name

- #livinglikealocal
- #locallife
- #locavore
- #shoplocal
- #supportlocal
- #localbrand
- #eatlocal
- #drinklocal
- #localbusiness
- #handmade
- #homemade

14

TRY SOMETHING THAT SCARES YOU

This is a highly subjective topic that only you can answer: What scares you? For some, it may be public speaking. For others, it could be something as simple as watching a scary movie. Whatever makes your heart race and your palms sweat, college is the place to conquer at least one of those fears. Or, at the very least, look it square in the eye before turning and heading for the hills.

Just to clarify, we do not mean willfully doing something potentially life-threatening. We are not advocating walking home alone from the bars at closing time and purposely ducking through every dark alley, or going to the zoo and trying to high five one of the lions. No, we mean something to get your heart pumping that you will look back on and say, "I can't believe I did that!" To simplify things, let's concentrate on the extreme thrill-seeking adventures. You know, the ones that will make your parents wish they could still ground you.

Some ideas to get you thinking:

- sky diving

- white-water rafting

- bungee jumping

- hang gliding

- surfing

- scuba diving

- roller coasters

- snowmobiling

- wind surfing

- jet skiing

- cliff diving

Starting to get the idea? Chances are one or more of these will be available in your area. If not, keep them in mind the next time you're on spring or summer break. You may surprise yourself at how fearless you can be and have one crazy story to tell everyone about as well! Just be sure to warn the parents before showing them the pictures. Have a blast, but stay safe!

SUGGESTED HASHTAGS

- The activity you're doing

- #adventure

- #thrill

- #heartracing
- #heartpumping
- #fears
- #conqueringfears
- #adrenaline
- #summerbreak
- #fearless
- #nofear
- #whatamIdoing
- #why
- #whynot

15

EXPERIMENT WITH YOUR LOOK

College is all about trying out new things, so why not do something daring with your appearance? Now is the time to try a dramatic hairstyle you've always wanted, whether it's a cute pixie cut, fabulously long hair extensions, or dyeing it hot pink. For you fellows, why not try growing out your facial hair, or if you've been rocking that beard for too long, shaving it all off! You fellows can get in on dyeing your hair too. You know there's an inner punk inside you just waiting to come out!

Think back to the last time you were flipping through a magazine or watching a movie and thought "I wonder if I could pull that off" when you saw an actor's hairstyle. Well, college is the perfect place to test that! If you don't have the extra cash to go down to the salon, see if your town has a local beauty college. Students need the practice and will cut your hair for an insanely low price. Yeah they're not professionals (yet), but c'mon! Where's your sense of adventure?

A piercing is also a great way to shake up your style. Whether it's that nineties throwback nose ring you've always had a sneaking suspicion would look amazing on you or an extra hole in your ear, now is the time to try something that high school you would never dare. If you're feeling extra brave you can even commit to a tattoo as a permanent reminder of the amazing time you had. Just make sure it's something that is meaningful to you and you won't be sick of in 10 years, and that you're totally sober when you make your decision. No one wants to wake up with embarrassing song lyrics or a shamrock permanently etched on their ass. (This seemed to happen to people a lot around St. Patrick's Day!)

What do you have to lose (besides looking silly)? It's college, you're supposed to be making impulsive choices!

SUGGESTED HASHTAGS

- #fashion
- #diy
- #mystyle
- #originalme
- #oneofakind
- #tattoo
- #newdo
- #shorthairdontcare

- #longhairdontcare
- #pinkhairdontcare
- #bold
- #salon
- #redlips
- #looks
- #newlook
- #newyearnewme

16

EXPLORE LOCAL MUSEUMS

It's not too hard to find a little bit of culture if you step outside your college bubble. Every city, large and small, has a variety of museums for locals and tourists alike.

If you're going to college in big cities like New York, Los Angeles, Seattle, or Austin, you've got some of the best museums in the country in your own backyard.

If you're going to a college in a small town, you will still have museums around. They'll just be more niche-oriented and might focus on the town's history or something quirky, like the National Yo-Yo Museum in Chico, CA. The small town of our alma mater has five museums within walking distance of campus.

To find what's available in your college town, just hop on the Internet for a quick Google search. You'll be able to find hours and admission fees in just a couple of clicks.

Some of the museums may be based on donations only, others could have a flat admission fee. Many will likely offer student discounts as well. Do your research and you'll see most museums are an inexpensive way to spend a day. All of them will be worth exploring at least once, if not to get a little culture, but also to learn about the local history of the town where you reside.

Once you and your friends pick a museum and/or an exhibit you want to see, make sure to bring a fully-charged phone to capture your day. Some museums might have Snapchat filters. Others will have Instagram hashtags. You may discover a new artist to love, and you'll want to share their artwork on social media.

SUGGESTED HASHTAGS

- The exhibit
- The name of the museum
- The name of the artist
- The name of the artwork
- The type of art (sculpture, painting, digital, etc.)
- #artselfie
- #artwatchers
- #partsofpaintings (When you're sharing details up close.)
- #streetart
- #explore
- #contemporary
- #modern
- #museumselfieday

- #museumselfie
- #victorian
- #artmatters
- #arthistory
- #paintingoftheday
- #abstract
- #culture

17

STUDY ABROAD

Whether you go for one semester, a whole year, or just a summer session, studying abroad is a life-changing experience. Meet with your school's advisors to learn about the various programs available to you in your major. They'll be able to answer all your questions and help you get signed up to go.

Here are a few things to know about studying abroad.

1. Most students study abroad during their junior year because it's the most convenient. At this point, you've finished most of your undergraduate requirements, and you haven't yet hit the stress of senior year and preparing for graduation.

2. When you sign up for your overseas classes, make sure the credits will be accepted and applied to your transcripts.

3. You will need a passport. If you don't already have one, start the process early to apply for one. The process is long, expensive, and requires a lot of paperwork, including your birth certificate, two passport-sized photos, certified identification (like a driver's license), a passport application,

and the payment. Once you get your passport, make a copy of it for your parents to keep safe.

4. The best timing to purchase your airfare is about three months in advance. Set up alerts on travel websites like Kayak or Airfare Watchdog to get notices when prices drop.

5. Learn about the currency exchange rate and prepare a budget in advance. Spending can spiral out of control before you know it.

6. Check with your bank about overseas fees and see if they will have a local bank you will be able to use while traveling.

7. You might get homesick. But don't let it take over. Acknowledge that you miss home, and remember you are on an adventure.

8. Download WhatsApp on your smartphone to be able to stay in touch with the people back home for free.

9. Use every weekend to explore a new place. If you are going to Europe, it is so easy and affordable to get around to the different countries.

10. Try as many new foods as you can—even if they sound weird.

11. There is a certain beauty that can be found when you get lost.

SUGGESTED HASHTAGS

- You may want to create your own hashtag for your whole trip. One easy suggestion is to combine your name with the country (e.g., #SarahTakesFrance #JoshTakesSpain #CarolynTakesBrazil).

- The cities you visit

- The sites you see

- The names of your schools

- The semester and year of your travels
- #studyabroad
- #wanderlust
- #travel
- #wannabewanderer
- #tourist
- #vacation
- #globetrotter
- #explore
- #adventure
- #ig_travel
- #traveladdict
- #seetheworld
- #studentlifestyles
- #studenttravel
- #educationabroad

18

GO ON A SPRING BREAK VACATION

Beaches. Parties. Alcohol. College students. The four ingredients necessary for an epic spring break vacation.

To plan the trip of a lifetime, you'll need to start early. Last-minute deals do not exist. Prices go up as spring break gets closer because these destinations know the students are coming and space is limited.

To get the best deals, start researching as soon as you decide where to go. There are a number of websites offering all-inclusive resort packages (flights not included) as early as August. You'll need to budget ahead of time as most trips could reach (or even exceed) $1,000 when everything is calculated.

The perk of staying at all-inclusive resorts is the variety of what's included for one flat price—food, drinks, private beach access, numerous pools, and more.

Plan to go with a solid group of friends you really trust. Don't invite the drama queen—she will bring her tantrums with her. Go with the group of friends who are responsible and whose party style you know. You don't want to get stuck playing mom all week to the one friend who doesn't know her alcohol limit.

If you are heading to spring break single, hookups are bound to happen. Students from all across the country are traveling to the same locations you are. You are sure to have a fling with someone you will likely never see again. Proceed with caution and use protection.

Just remember, spring break should be three things: fun, unforgettable, and carefree.

TOP 5 LOCAL DESTINATIONS

1. Las Vegas, Nevada
2. Miami, Florida
3. Daytona Beach, Florida
4. Panama City Beach, Florida
5. South Padre Island, Texas

TOP 5 INTERNATIONAL DESTINATIONS

1. Puerto Vallarta, Mexico
2. Cancun, Mexico
3. Nassau, Bahamas

4. Punta Cana, Dominican Republic

5. Cabo San Lucas, Mexico

SUGGESTED HASHTAGS

- Create a hashtag for your trip. Maybe use the initials of everyone's first name. Or create a name for your group.

- Your location

- #springbreak

- #bestfriends

- #bestphotos

- #spoiled

- #lifestyle

- #enjoying

- #partyincoming

- #instatravel

- #partytime

- #beachside

- #yolo

19

GO TO EUROPE

If you are unable to study abroad, don't fret. Europe is still calling your name!

Not sure when or where to go? Well, friend, there's a reason why winter breaks are more than a month long. You can take a two-week trip to Europe during the holidays, which is a wonderful time to visit. Or you can head overseas during summer break and backpack through a couple of countries.

If you have a friend that is studying abroad, make a plan to visit them and block out time in your schedules to travel together. You can easily hit a few different destinations in one trip by spending a day or two in each city.

Where should you stay? Hostels. You're young, you don't need a luxury boutique hotel every night. Plus, most people staying in hostels are all around the same age. You'll make fast friends with those who are also staying at the same place. You'll get to share your travel stories: where you've been, and where you're going. You may even decide to change your travel plans to buddy up with your new pals. They might have suggestions on places to go or things to do.

The excitement with traveling is the unexpected. You don't know whose path you'll cross and where that path will lead you. You could make friends for life.

If you are hoping to go to Europe but you don't have a lot of funds for traveling around, you can head there to work. Maybe you can find an internship during summer break. Or you can look into a work abroad program. Through these programs, you can find temporary jobs and gigs that either pay you or offer free room and board in exchange for your help. Use your time off to explore other nearby sites or cities.

There are many ways to travel on a budget. You just have to be willing to do the research to find the best opportunities for you.

Did You Know? The drinking age in most European countries is 18. Check out page 145 on other places you can go where the drinking age is under 21.

SUGGESTED HASHTAGS

- The cities you visit

- The countries you visit

- The sites you see

- #cathedral

- #BigBen

- #eiffeltower
- #Gaudi
- #football
- #fishnchips
- #europe
- #eurotrip
- #beautifuldestinations
- #citylife
- #bridge
- #canals

20

HAVE A THEMED PARTY

First rule of theme parties: get a little more creative than adding "and Hoes" or "and Sluts" to the end of the theme name. Here are 25 themes you can use for your next costume party. We guarantee these will be a hit with your friends and that everyone will show up in costume!

1. **BEACH PARTY.** Swimsuits, grass skirts, Hawaiian shirts.

2. **STOPLIGHT.** Each guest wears the color that signifies their relationship status. Green = Single. Red = Taken. Yellow = Proceed with caution because it's complicated.

3. **BLACK LIGHT.** Replace all light bulbs with black lights. Get glow-in-the-dark decorations and highlighters. Everyone must wear a white shirt. Get creative with your artwork (someone will be drawing dicks) and doodle on everyone's shirt.

4. **DUCT TAPE PARTY.** Outfits must be made out of duct tape.

5. **CASINO PARTY.** Blackjack, poker, roulette. Let the games begin!

6. **DECADES.** You either pick a decade as the theme, or each person can dress up from the decade of their choice.

7. **VIDEO GAME THEME PARTY.** This party will need a couple of different rooms for each gaming station. Guests will play a different video game in each room.

8. **FAMOUS WHO.** Each guest dresses up in a recognizable costume (celebrity or character), and everyone must guess the person. Get it wrong and you have to take a shot.

9. **PAJAMA PARTY.** PJs for everyone!

10. **SEVEN DEADLY SINS.** Dress up as pride, envy, gluttony, lust, sloth, wrath, or greed.

11. **SUPERHERO PARTY.** Grab your cape, it'll be a battle of the superheroes.

12. **UGLY SWEATER.** This theme is best for the holiday season.

13. **ALPHABET SOUP.** Dress up as something that starts with the same letter of your first name.

14. **TOGA PARTY.** A classic.

15. **AMERICA.** All things USA.

16. **WHEN I GROW UP...** Dress up as your future self in 5, 10, 20, or 40 years.

17. **LETTER PARTY.** Pick a letter and everyone must dress up as something that starts with that letter.

18. **GRAFFITI PARTY.** Very similar to a Black Light party. Everyone must wear a white shirt. This time, the artwork is with sharpies. Great for going-away parties.

19. **ABC PARTY.** Anything but Cups. Bring your own drinking container. Or Anything but Clothes—get creative in assembling your outfit.

20. **ANY MOVIE OR TV SHOW.** The more characters, the better. Think *Game of Thrones* or *The Walking Dead*.

21. **REALITY TV SHOW.** Dress up as a character who belongs on a reality show, like *Real Housewives*, *The Bachelor*, or *Jersey Shore*.

22. **THE FUTURE.** What will life be like in the year 2075? You decide.

23. **HIGH SCHOOL STEREOTYPES.** Dress up as a cheerleader, the nerd, a drama queen, or the jock.

24. **RISKY BUSINESS.** You may not know the movie, but you know the outfit—oversized button-down shirt, white underwear, white socks. Play "Old Time Rock and Roll" on repeat.

25. **ANYTHING FOR A BUCK.** Use fake money, and your guests exchange bills with each other for whatever they want—whether it's a dance or a body shot.

SUGGESTED HASHTAGS

• Create a Snapchat filter for everyone to use during the party, and create a party hashtag.

• The party theme

• #college

• #parties

• #dancing

• #raging

• #vodka

• #drink

• #cocktails

• #fun

- #gettingwild
- #dressedforfun
- #celebrations

21

GO ON A DAY TRIP

It is totally normal to feel bored by your town. We've all been there. Every day feels like the same ol' thing. And sometimes, there really is nothing to do! That's when you need to break daily routine.

The same thing day after day is exhausting. It's when you change up your schedule and your surroundings that you make the most memories. So when you feel adventure calling your name, take a day trip. Grab your friends, hop in a car, and great ready to explore. Follow these dos and don'ts and you'll have an incredible day checking out a new place.

1. **DO** go to a neighboring town. Even if you are only driving 15 or 20 minutes away, a new town will feel new. You'll find new places to go and new things to do. And you won't have to stress about getting there.

2. **DON'T** forget to research. If you're going on a day trip, you should know a little bit about your final destination. Do you need reservations at the restaurant? What's parking like? Can you explore on foot?

3. **DO** turn your day trip into a weekend getaway. Use apps like Airbnb or HotelTonight to find an affordable place to stay the night.

4. **DON'T** drink too much. If you need to drive back to your town, remember to be responsible.

5. **DO** look into where you can go using public transportation. If you don't have a car, don't fret. Buses and trains can get you there and back (on the cheap!) without having to worry about traffic, gas, or tolls.

6. **DON'T** travel too far. Keep your driving distance within two hours each way. Anything more than that and it's too exhausting to go there and back in one day.

7. **DO** think like a tourist. Look at this town with new eyes. You'll discover local gems and unique charms that make these cities so great.

8. **DON'T** forget the essentials. Between GPS, Yelp, and taking photos, you'll be using your smartphone a lot. You may need an external charger to keep your battery going. Bring snacks for the road. You never know when hunger will strike. And bring a sweater or jacket in case it gets chilly at night.

9. **DO** treat yourself. Enjoy a decadent dessert. Splurge on that special knick-knack that you must have. These are the moments that make these adventures unforgettable.

SUGGESTED HASHTAGS

- #daytrip
- #travel
- #instatravel
- #travelgram

- #tourist
- #tourism
- #vacation
- #trip
- #adventure
- #theresnoplacelikehome
- #hotfuninthesummertime
- #explore

22

FIND A PLACE TO WATCH THE SUNRISE

Share a picture of a sunrise and it just might become your most liked post. With some light Google searching, you should be able to find recommendations on great vista points around town to see the sunrise. Once you know where you are going, follow these tips to really soak up the beauty of a sunrise.

1. **WAKE UP EARLY.** And we mean early. You have to get up when it's still dark out! It might be easier in the fall or winter when the sun rises later in the day. Set your alarm for 5 a.m. or so, depending on how far you need to drive.

2. **DRESS WARM.** If you go in the fall/winter, the mornings can be a bit chilly. Pack a blanket too, for extra coziness.

3. **PACK SOME FOOD.** Make some hot chocolate, bring some fruit and/or some doughnuts to enjoy when you get there.

4. **HOP IN A CAR AND HEAD TO YOUR VIEWING POINT.** Sit where you can see the sun. Remember, the sun rises in the east and sets in the west.

5. **RELAX.** If you go with a group, try to keep the loud chitchat to a minimum. The world is so calm and quiet this early in the morning, so you should embrace it and welcome the peace.

6. **WATCH THE BEAUTY IN FRONT OF YOU.** Take note of all the different colors, from red to orange to pink to purple. Look at the whole picture, the sky, the clouds. Take a picture if you'd like. But remember to be present.

7. **LISTEN.** You'll hear birds waking up. You might hear water from a nearby creek. You might hear the wind rustling through the trees.

8. **SMILE.** The world is a magical place!

SUGGESTED HASHTAGS

- Your city
- Your spot
- #sunset
- #sunrise
- #sun
- #sunsetporn
- #pretty
- #beautiful
- #red
- #orange
- #pink
- #sky
- #skyporn

- #cloudporn
- #nature
- #clouds
- #horizon
- #photooftheday
- #gorgeous
- #warm
- #view
- #night
- #morning
- #sunrays
- #landscape
- #earth
- #moments
- #iwishyouwerehere

THINGS THAT YOU'LL TREASURE YEARS FROM NOW

It's hard to think about the future-future when you're in college. Right now, you're in a bubble where you don't have to face the (sometimes harsh) realities of adulting. Maybe you're still on the family plan for your cell phone coverage. Maybe your parents help you with your rent payments. Or maybe you've made an agreement that you don't have to work part-time jobs while you go to school. No matter who you are, you are in transition from being seen as a kid to becoming someone who can fend for themselves. To go full truth-bomb on you, this is the last time you will ever have as few responsibilities as you do right now. Soak. It. Up.

And that's why we wrote this chapter. The to-do list items in this section will tap into the nostalgia that "future you" will have for "college you." In five, ten, or 15 years, you'll still think about when you and your friends had the best night ever. And when you're 40 or 50 (it's a scary thought, we know!), you'll realize just how hot you were at 20. Take as many pictures as you can right now. You'll want to capture these moments. Help out future you by turning memories into tangible items you can delight in for years to come.

TAKE PICTURES, PRINT, AND FRAME THEM

Thanks to smartphones we're all amateur photographers now, able to snap a pic and share it anytime, anywhere. But why not preserve some of those shots rather than just letting them pile up on your phone? Let's say you go to a party with friends, have a fabulous time, take tons of selfies and group shots, pick the perfect filters, and share on social media while tagging your friends (only the flattering ones, please). Then, after enjoying all the likes and comments, you promptly forget about them. Why not dig out the best group photos, artsy nature shots, and candid snaps and actually print them? Yes, like make physical prints.

You need pictures to put on your bedroom/dorm walls anyway. So why not print out some fun shots of you and your friends living your best college life? You can have a whole wall devoted to your hilarious college hijinks, a fun and cheap way to decorate and personalize your living space.

Printing out and framing photos is also a meaningful, low-cost gift idea for friends and family. For birthdays or Christmas, nothing will impress more than a thoughtful photo in a nice picture frame. There are also several websites like Shutterfly that can help you compile cute photo books and other great gift ideas.

No matter how awesome our phones are and how many new flashy photo apps come out, there's just something special and permanent feeling about actually holding a physical print in your hand. Your future self with thank you for capturing the unforgettable college moments and making sure they last.

START A BLOG

Between schoolwork and screwing around on your phone outside of classes, you probably already spend a lot of time online. But besides the requisite entertainment and social media sites, why not make your mark by starting your own website? Whether it's as simple as a Tumblr blog showcasing your rambling thoughts and hilarious gifs or a more seriously designed portfolio showing off your professional work, publishing a personal site will give you a chance to develop some new skills, build your online presence, or just carve out a corner of the web that's just for you outside of school and your IRL activities.

One major benefit to having your own blog: you can have a space to rant or vent about personal stuff with as much anonymity as you want, without your entire extended family seeing it on Facebook or Twitter.

Having a blog is not just about writing. You are controlling every aspect of the layout, design, and content, which means you will be learning useful technical skills as you figure out the different features. And the more skills you have in your arsenal, the more impressive your resume will be, post-college.

SUGGESTIONS

1. Have a brilliant idea for a site or app that could actually be useful? Develop that shit and become the next Zuckerberg!

2. Share your art! Build a site to showcase your writing, photography, Lego sculpture building, cat paintings, whatever—just put it out there.

3. Use your website to network! Reach out to people you admire who may be able to help you build your career or give you helpful advice after college.

MAKE A PLAYLIST OF YOUR COLLEGE JAMS

Nothing can transport you back to a specific moment of time in your life like music. Hearing a song you haven't heard in years can instantly bring you back to whatever time or place you were in when the song was first played. So why not make a time capsule to your future self and create a playlist of your college jams?

What songs are in regular rotation on your way to school? What are the hit songs that are getting played to death? What's considered the "song of the summer"? What are the hit dance songs that get played every Saturday night at the clubs? Compile them all in one playlist and be transported back instantly to your awkward, nervous freshman year or your more confident, self-assured senior year. Don't just choose whatever is a hit on the radio this year. Include the songs that you're personally obsessed with, regardless of if it is new or years old.

You'll want to bust this mix out at a future gathering with your old college friends for sure!

26

GET MENTIONED IN THE SCHOOL NEWSPAPER

Most universities have school newspapers. Some are weeklies, some might print twice a week, others might be online only. Wherever you are, there are student reporters covering campus news.

You might spot the student journalists at the big Friday night game, or you might see them wandering campus for interviews. Find them when and where breaking news happens. A fire on campus? They'll be there. A campus protest? They'll be there. St. Patrick's Day shenanigans in your college town? They'll be there.

Like any media outlet, some of those stories they produce will be good, uplifting, and inspiring. Other stories will be the bad news we're used to seeing everyday—crimes, accidents, scandals.

Let's hope that when your name is printed in the paper's pages, it will be to celebrate one of your incredible accomplishments. Because at one point during your college years, you will do something that is newsworthy. Maybe your club exceeded its fundraising goals. Maybe you won the election to become student body president. Maybe you landed an incredible, once-in-a-lifetime internship. All of these achievements should be celebrated and could make for a feel-good story.

If you know when the article about you will run, be sure to grab copies of the paper to send to all your relatives. You know your parents and grandparents will be thrilled to see your picture and name in the paper. They'll show it to all their friends and neighbors, eager to brag about you any chance they get.

27

WRITE A LETTER TO YOUR FUTURE SELF THAT YOU'LL READ WHEN YOU GRADUATE

Think back to your first day of high school. Now think back to your last day of high school. You changed a lot in those four years, right? That won't even prepare you for how much you'll grow up during your four or five years of undergrad.

You'll go through some of the most life-changing experiences, including having (and maybe losing) your first love, living with a significant other for the first time, or maybe having to learn how to handle 12 weeks with a professor you don't like or who doesn't like you. In short, college will test you, and you won't always know if you passed or failed.

To take stock of who you were and who you will become, write a letter to your future self. Stash it away until the day you graduate.

What should you write in the letter? Here are some questions you can answer:

1. What are your dreams for your future self?

2. What are your fears about the future?

3. What are your goals for the first year after you graduate? 5 years after? 10 years after?

4. What do you hope you learn about yourself in college?

5. What mistakes are you scared you'll make?

6. What are you scared you'll regret?

7. What do you think will be your favorite memories of college after you graduate?

8. What are your hopes and dreams for your friendships made during college?

9. What do you hope you'll know by the time you graduate?

10. What's on your college bucket list?

11. What encouragement do you want to give yourself before you enter the real world?

12. How do you think you'll feel about graduation?

13. What do you think you'll miss most about college?

After you finish the letter, seal it in an envelope and write the date you'll open it. Store it in a safe place until that future day arrives.

28

CALL YOUR FAMILY

You have a smartphone. Put that baby to use. With technology like FaceTime and Skype, it has never been easier to stay in touch with loved ones. Getting to see each other's faces makes the distance feel smaller.

A quick FaceTime call will help put your parents' anxieties at ease, as they'll get to see that you are capable of taking care of yourself. They'll see what your life is like when you're away at college. While you're on camera, you can give them different tours—of your dorm or apartment; your favorite places on campus; your favorite dining hall; and where you like to go during your free time. You can even introduce your friends.

Who should you call and how often? This will depend on your relationships and what works best for each dynamic. The following are just suggestions; feel free to adjust as you please.

1. **PARENTS:** FaceTime them at least once a month. Call them at least once a week. Text and email a few times a week.

2. **GRANDPARENTS:** Call them at least once a month. Maybe more if you are really close to them.

3. **SIBLINGS:** Text constantly—it's probably the preferred method of communication for you both. Call them a couple times a month, typically if you have a crazy story to share. If you are close in age (within a couple years, both in college at the same time), you'll start to notice how your relationship is changing. It will include less picking on one another and more adult conversations.

You must also remember that keeping these calls up can come with a number of perks. If you say something subtle to Grandma and Grandpa about how you can't afford to go to a concert that all your friends are going to, we're going to bet that they offer to send you some money. If you casually say to Mom that you desperately miss her chocolate chip cookies, keep an eye on your mailbox. She just might send you a little care package. Use their feelings of missing you and the distance between you to your advantage. You can thank us later.

THINGS YOU
WON'T REGRET

Are you ready to challenge yourself? What follows are bucket list items that will take you outside your bubble and will push you out of your comfort zone. These are risks worth taking. Trust us, we know from experience.

While all 101 items in this book could technically be categorized as "things you won't regret," the ones here specifically will help you grow—they'll challenge you to become smarter, more confident, more gracious and selfless.

When you take a class outside of your major, you'll stimulate your brain in new ways. When you thank a professor for all he/she has done for you, you'll learn the true power of gratitude. When you hook up somewhere on campus, you will understand more about your sexuality. And when you attend a student protest, you'll learn about equality and the importance of using your voice. It can be easy to say no to any of these experiences. In the moment, you may not see the actual benefit or outcome. But afterward, you'll realize exactly how these instances brought about a new aspect to who you are.

GO OUT WITH SOMEONE DIFFERENT FROM YOUR USUAL TYPE

By now you may have noticed a trend in this book: we are a big proponent of getting out of your comfort zone and trying new experiences, especially during your college years. One of the biggest ways you can do that? Make an effort to date, or at least get to know, someone different from your usual "type."

Have you ever dated outside your immediate social group? Ever branched out and gotten to know someone completely different from you? Odds are, probably not. High school can be a rigid place where it's easy to stick to your respective cliques and not bother to branch out and get to know people in other groups. Well, college is the perfect place to break that habit and meet new people.

Try dating a bookish type if you normally date jocks, or vice versa. Take a chance on letting a friend set you up—

you never know who you might connect with. When taking classes outside of your major, check out the other students. Go to campus functions that are outside of your usual interests and make an effort to strike up a conversation with an interesting-looking person. Maybe there's someone you never would have run into otherwise that might be fun to get to know. If you do the online dating thing, take a chance on someone who you might normally pass on because they don't meet all your rigid expectations. So they're not a tall, blonde philosophy major who loves Star Wars? So what, give it a shot! You may be pleasantly surprised.

30

SET UP A GROUP OUTING WITH PEOPLE FROM YOUR MAJOR

Quick: What's a fun way to increase your social circle and help with your academic experience? Answer: make an effort to meet and bond with people in your major! Think about it: you already have something in common with a ton of different students from all walks of life who come from all over the place. Their unique perspectives and points of view will perhaps help you see aspects of your major in a different way. Once you get to know some of them, you can form study groups, share notes and tips on different professors and projects, and have people to bitch to about that one lousy professor or that killer assignment.

Odds are, taking shared classes and collaborating on group projects will break the ice somewhat. But to really get to know people and form a bond outside the classroom, we recommend organizing a group outing somewhere off campus.

The trick to a successful gathering is to keep it casual, since everyone is still getting acquainted. This can be as simple as doing a spontaneous happy hour meetup after class or even a BBQ over the weekend in a local park (see page 233). You can also make an online group for people to join, through Facebook or another social platform.

However, if you decide to go about befriending people within your major, the payoff will be worth the effort and make you feel like you have allies in a sometimes alienating environment. Plus, the connections you make in college can sometimes come in very handy down the road, well after graduation.

31

READ BOOKS IN UNFAMILIAR GENRES

We know, we know, you already have a ton of reading to do in college! So why seek out more books to read on top of that?! Well, hopefully you've made it a habit to read as a hobby and a fun pastime; if not, it's never too late to learn to love a good book. Reading is a great, cheap way to unwind and forget about your life for a while. And unlike passively watching TV, reading will engage your brain and expand your imagination and vocabulary, and make you a more interesting person in general. Can you tell we're big fans of reading?

If you are already an avid reader, good for you! Why not branch out and explore other genres you may be unfamiliar with? Ask your favorite professor for a recommendation, explore the library and grab a random book off the shelf and crack it open, or organize a book club with your friends and take turns recommending favorites.

Your college library is, of course, a great resource, but be sure to check out local bookstores as well. They often have talks by visiting authors and have pretty decent used book selections, so you can take a chance on an unknown book without breaking the bank. Thrift stores and yard sales are good for this reason as well.

Stumped on what to read next? Try going to a bookstore employee and asking, "What's the book you're most excited about selling right now?" Even if it doesn't sound interesting or if it's in a genre you're unfamiliar with, get it anyway. You may be pleasantly surprised. Happy reading!

32

ORGANIZE A STUDENT PROTEST

Hey, who's that guy yelling into a megaphone on the campus quad? Odds are, it's a student activist trying to rally support for his or her pet cause. Hey, you should join in! You owe it to yourself to really have a well-rounded college experience and get in on the action of a good old-fashioned student protest!

So think about it for a minute: Is there a cause or problem in society that you're passionate about or want to learn more about? Odds are, there's already a group of like-minded students that have formed a group about it. Ask to take a leadership position and help organize the next protest. You can make signs, get signatures on petitions, hang up fliers, call the local media, then when the time comes, get up there with a megaphone and let your voice be heard!

Okay, if the idea of doing any of that sounds far from your scene, then consider at least showing up for a protest if it's a cause you care about. Showing support and solidarity is just as important as being the ones making the noise.

Plot twist: you hear about a protest/rally for something that you do not agree with. Show up anyway! Be the dissenting voice if there is a gathering for something you find offensive. If you see the KKK, men's rights activists, or another abhorrent group setting up for a rally, stick around and give 'em a hearty "Fuck you!" Start a counter-protest to their shenanigans.

Did You Know? The first recorded student protest in the USA took place at Harvard University in 1766. The students revolted against the less-than-appealing dining options in the cafeteria, and the incident was dubbed "The Butter Rebellion."

33

ORGANIZE FOR A PLAY OR IMPROV GROUP

If you've ever been onstage for any kind of performance, you know there is nothing quite like the adrenaline and rush of hearing applause for the first time. If you've never done a play, sketch show, or anything like that, why not give it a shot? Go to an audition for one of the school plays or try out for the local improv or sketch comedy troupe. If you're feeling really confident, arrange a slot at an open mic night and do a stand-up routine. Who knows, you just might find your new calling in life. Or you might find the experience pants-shittingly terrifying and curse us for ever even suggesting you do that. But how will you know if you don't try?

Do your research on the type of audition you plan to attend. Is it a general audition? Cold read? Improv? If you're unclear on how to prepare, get in contact with someone involved in the production and ask them.

If the show is a musical, expect to have a monologue and at least 16 bars of a Broadway song memorized.

If it is a cold reading audition, this means you will get a part of the script, sight unseen until audition day, to act out in front of the auditioners. Often it is with you and another partner, or it can be a monologue.

An improvisational audition is usually the most casual setting, where the auditioners will ask you to improv different scenarios and situations to see how quick on your feet you can be with new material.

Try putting yourself on stage at least once. Even if it doesn't work out, you won't regret it in the long run. Break a leg!

34

SEEK OUT NEW MUSIC

Are you stuck in a rut, music-wise? Is your iPod full of the same songs you've been jamming to since high school? Then you're in luck. College is the perfect backdrop to expand your musical knowledge and discover new genres. Ask friends for recommendations and give them a try with an open mind. Share playlists with your friends via a streaming service like Spotify or go super old school and burn each other CDs or mixed tapes. Go to concerts for bands and musicians you've never heard of; you may realize you have an affinity for a totally new genre of music, like bluegrass, hip-hop, or punk. Colleges often have some big-name acts come through and play on campus for cheap or even free. If you want to save money, look into volunteering as an usher for on-campus concerts. You get to see the show for free! Your campus radio station most likely has some unique and underground music that you won't hear on mainstream radio as well.

If you travel to any music festivals on spring break, be sure to catch as many different bands as possible.

Extra credit: Burn a CD or share a personalized playlist of your new favorite songs for a crush. This old-school courting technique is a classic for a reason!

Did You Know? According to Rolling Stone, the college towns with the best music scenes (ranked by number of venues, record stores, and college radio) are:

- Seattle, WA
- Austin, TX
- Nashville, TN
- San Francisco, CA
- Athens, GA
- Minneapolis, MN

35

EXPLORE YOUR SPIRITUAL SIDE

However you refer to it, spirituality/religion/faith (or lack thereof) is obviously very personal and often something you're raised with based on your family's beliefs and cultures. When you're in college and away from the familiar, why not use this as an opportunity to explore what spirituality really means to you? Whether that means joining an interfaith campus group, attending an unfamiliar religious service, or taking some courses to learn the history behind other belief systems (Hindu? Islam? Early Christianity? Wicca?), this is a great opportunity to expand your mind and gain a deeper understanding of what people believe and why.

Consider taking a history of religion class to broaden your understanding of how modern religions came to be. It would be a good way to get some elective credits out of the way and gain a greater understanding of the world.

36

BUY YOUR PROFESSOR
A DRINK

Professors are human beings just like the rest of us. They need their downtime, and occasionally, a night out to drink a beer or three, especially after having to teach all of us. So don't be surprised to see one of them the next time you're out at a bar. When this happens, why not do the ultimate "We're not in high school anymore" move and buy them a drink?

Not only will you score some brownie points with them, but it'll remind you that you have more in common with your professors than you originally thought. You are both adults, and they were once college students like you.

If they are with friends, then obviously don't linger, but if they are alone and seem receptive, don't be afraid to sit down and share a drink with them. Leave the classroom questions about papers and homework and stuff for visiting them during their office hours (covered in Utilize Your Professor's Office Hours on page 199). Ask them how they got started in teaching and what college was like for them. They may have some valuable advice on how to pick a career path or navigate your college experience. This is especially helpful if the professor happens to be teaching in a field you would like to make a career out of when you graduate. In that case, get as much advice as you can from them—you could be amazed at what you can learn.

37

EXPERIMENT WITH NEW CLOTHING STYLES

Have you ever wondered what a particular clothing style would look on you? Have you ever had the urge to mix up your wardrobe and try something bold and daring? Well, you're in luck, because college is the perfect place to do that! You're away from home for the first time, where no one knows who you are. You can try out as many new looks as you want and dress like you wouldn't have dared to in high school. So what are you waiting for?

Okay, so a big hurdle is obviously the cost. You most likely can't afford to get yourself a whole new wardrobe. Luckily there are many cheap/free ways to expand your clothing collection.

1. Shop online at websites like Craigslist, Amazon, etc., for cheap clothing deals. Many name-brand stores offer online coupons and other deals.

2. Have a clothing swap with friends. Invite them over and have them bring any clothes they no longer want. Then everyone digs through each other's cast-offs and takes what they want.

3. Thrift stores are your friend! It may take some patience, but you can find some amazing deals for dirt cheap.

4. Don't forget about yard sales. They can be a great source for cheap clothes and accessories.

5. If you have an article of clothing that still fits you but you no longer like, consider changing it up into a new style. You can dye shirts a new color, turn jeans into cute shorts—the possibilities are endless. Don't be too hasty in chucking your old threads!

6. Accessories are a cheap way to ease into a new style. Hats, belts, jewelry, and shoes can all help you formulate a new look without breaking the bank.

Above all, be bold and fearless when it comes to trying out a new style. It may not work out, but you can at least know you went for it. And the pictures will be hilarious when you look back on them years later!

38

MAKE A MOVE ON YOUR CRUSH

So you've been scoping out that guy/gal. You know the one, the person that makes you a tongue-tied mess when you find yourself in their presence. What the hell is up with that? You may have already realized this, but you've got yourself a big ol' crush. The next question, of course, is what do you plan to do about it?

I feel like you already know where this is going. Unless you haven't picked up on the general theme of this book yet, here it is: Take a risk! Go for it!

Yeah, okay FINE. It takes a certain amount of finesse and courage to go up and start talking to your crush, especially if you want it to go well. Here are a few scenarios and some simple conversation starters and pick-up lines to get you started.

WALKING AROUND CAMPUS

EASY: "Excuse me, do you know where (building name) is located?"

ADVANCED: "Hey, would you mind walking me to my car? It's getting late and I don't like walking alone."

PIMP STATUS: "You're so cute, you made me forget my pickup line."

EXTRA CREDIT: "Do you have a moment to take a survey?" Hand them your phone with the New Contact screen open.

AT THE BAR OR CLUB

EASY: "I've never been here before, what should I order?"

ADVANCED: "I can read palms; give me your hand and I'll tell your future." Write your phone number on their palm.

P-I-M-P: "My friends over there bet $20 each that there's no way I could get your number. Wanna go out to dinner with their money?"

AT THE LIBRARY

EASY: "Hey, aren't you in (name of class)? Mind if I peek at your notes from yesterday's lecture?"

ADVANCED: "Oh, it looks like we grabbed the same book! Wanna start a book club?"

TOO HOT, HOT DAMN: "Hey, I need your opinion. I'm going on a blind date and I'm really nervous. Do you have any tips so I don't look like an idiot?" After the tips are provided, test out one of the moves then and there.

Take a risk and put yourself out there. If you get shot down, at least you'll know that you took a chance. And when the next crush comes around, you'll be more prepared than ever!

39

HAVE A FRIEND WITH BENEFITS

Let's be honest, sometimes you want the perks of a relationship without having to actually, you know, be in one. And by perks we mean sex. Hence the reason Friends with Benefits came to be. This type of situation is not for everyone, but if you want to give it a try, here is a primer on navigating it successfully:

1. **DO** be honest and upfront, every step of the way. The last thing you want is to step into a FWB situation and have the other person believe you are starting an actual relationship. Communicate! Make sure this is something both of you want equally.

2. **DON'T** get territorial or start questioning your friend about their other relationships. Jealousy has no place in a FWB situation. If they start doing that to you, time to have a frank and honest discussion or call the whole thing off.

3. **DO** assess the friendship. If this scenario goes south, will your friendship be able to withstand any potential hurt feelings or

awkwardness? Calculate the risk versus reward before taking the plunge.

4. **DON'T** do any cuddling/dates/presents/PDA, anything that screams "relationship." You are friends who occasionally get freaky, and if you both want more than that then just date already.

5. **DO BE SAFE!** Use condoms. This is true for any relationship, but especially FWB. Remember, neither of you are necessarily exclusive.

6. **DON'T** make it just about the sex. You started out as friends, so no reason why you can't continue to do friend things with this person.

Again, proceed with caution if this is your first time embarking on this kind of relationship. It definitely isn't for everyone, but for the busy college student who sometimes just wants to get laid without the whole "relationship" hassle, then a FWB situation might be just what you need.

40

HAVE A ONE-NIGHT STAND

Picture this: you're out with your friends at a bar or a party and you lock eyes with a hottie across the room. We've all had those "lust at first sight" moments. Let's say it progresses to chatting and hitting it off, leading you to ponder your next move for the evening: Will this be the night you have a one-night stand? Let's work through the pros and cons to determine how your night could end up.

PROS

1. It gives you an opportunity to figure out what pleases you most in bed and helps you figure out how to please your future partners as well. Practice makes perfect!

2. It's a way to get your rocks off without all the emotional baggage of a relationship.

3. The stress of endless midterms and hard classes wearing you down? Sex is a great stress relief!

4. Is your ego bruised from a recent breakup or being rejected by your crush? Nothing gets the confidence back faster than taking someone home at the end of the night.

5. Whether it turns out to be earthshaking, terrible, or meh, one thing is for sure: it'll make a good story to tell your friends.

CONS

1. Taking a stranger home, you increase your risk of STDs and unwanted pregnancy. You play the game, you better know all the risks, and take the necessary precautions!

2. You run the risk of bumping into your one-night stand in awkward situations (e.g., sitting next to you in class).

3. Sometimes, whether you like it or not, feelings get involved, leading to heartache and frustration.

4. The bottom line is, this person is a stranger. Going anywhere with someone you don't know can obviously lead to an unsafe situation. Use your best judgment, and when in doubt, go home with your friends instead!

Sometimes people have a one-night stand and realize that it's not for them. And that's okay! The point of college is to find out what you want and what works for you, in all aspects of life. So what are you waiting for? Go talk to the hottie!

SEND A FAVORITE PROFESSOR A THANK YOU NOTE WHEN YOU GRADUATE

The relationships you'll develop with professors will last long after you've left campus.

Your professors are some of the first real-world mentors you will have. They are standing on the sidelines cheering you on, eager to see you succeed after you've left the comfort and safety of your school's halls. Sometimes they will challenge you, and that may piss you off. Sometimes they'll go easy on you, because they know you need a break. But by graduation day, you'll want to thank them for pushing you, teaching you, and helping you grow up.

Teachers become teachers because they want to make an impact. They want to witness minds growing, expanding, and learning. Let them know they did a job well with a simple thank you note.

During your last week of classes before graduation, handwrite thank you notes to your favorite professors. You may have more than one. And if you only have one, that's okay too. Swing by their offices during their office hours for one last chat and to drop off the note.

What should you say in the note?

• Tell them about your favorite class.

• Tell them about your favorite lecture they gave.

• Maybe talk about a favorite class project and what you learned.

• Tell them what an influence they had on you.

• Tell them about a favorite discussion you two had during office hours.

• Tell them how their encouragement pushed you to try harder.

• Tell them how they helped you believe in your own dreams.

• Tell them thank you for all they did.

This one thank you note could be the start to a relationship that goes beyond the classroom and follows you into your adult life. You never know, you may end up staying in touch with one of your professors 10-plus years after you graduate, and you may even invite him to your wedding.

KISS SOMEONE YOU JUST MET

This one is only to be checked off when you are single and ready to mingle. We don't encourage cheating.

Let's set the scene. You're getting ready for a night out with your besties. The music is pumping, the pregame drinks are flowing, and you're picking out your best outfit. You know you want to look real fine when you step into the bar tonight. You want everyone to give you a two-syllable damn. (Don't we all?!)

As you're getting ready, you realize your mission of the night: to kiss a stranger.

Well, we're glad we can be here to help make this happen.

First, you'll want to inform your besties of your goal. You'll need them to keep their eyes out for potential kissing mates.

Next, once you roll up to the party (or bar or club), do a lap to see who is around. The stranger needs to be someone you have truly never met before. When you find the one to kiss, you'll know. The physical attraction will be undeniable. You'll lock eyes and just know the chemistry is there. You can start with a little casual chit-chat, but you'll both know talk is cheap. You're both really there for the steamy smooch session.

Kissing someone you just met is a thrill, but with anything, there are some rules. Here are our do's and don'ts:

1. **DO** have fresh breath.

2. **DON'T** chew gum. Spit it out.

3. **DO** mix it up between soft kisses and more passionate kisses.

4. **DON'T** wear red lipstick.

5. **DO** get a little frisky. Stroke your hand through his/her hair. Move your hand up and down his/her back.

6. **DON'T** use too much tongue.

7. **DO** stop talking. Just enjoy the makeout.

8. **DON'T** let your friends take pictures. They may haunt you.

9. **DO** try a tender lip bite while kissing.

10. **DON'T** lock your lips.

11. **DO** tell him/her they are a good kisser, but only if you mean it.

12. **DON'T** breathe into his/her mouth. Use your nose!

13. **DO** exchange numbers if you're interested in getting to know him/her better.

14. Last but not least, **DON'T** go home with them…yet.

43

HOOK UP SOMEWHERE ON CAMPUS

Sure, you can assume this will give you the steps to hooking up in the library without getting caught. But you'd be wrong. Instead, you'll find a list of places that have a little more risk in order to have a successful hookup—and after all, isn't it the risk that makes it all the more thrilling?

Whether it's a one-night stand (see page 103) or you and a significant other are looking to spice things up in your relationship, you can decide together which of the locales could actually work for a quickie. But, first, a couple of rules:

1. Make it quick—no tantric sex here.

2. Keep it quiet—the louder you are, the more likely someone will explore where that noise is coming from.

3. Wear clothes that can aid in a speedy fling. Dresses and skirts? Yes. Skinny jeans? Not so much.

4. Scout the location before you take action. While this may take some of the spontaneity out of the adventure, you'll want to

do your research on when each locale is at peak crowds and when it's practically deserted.

Follow these steps and you'll have a sexcapade you'll never forget.

31 PLACES WHERE YOU COULD POTENTIALLY HOOK UP ON CAMPUS

1. At your dorm.

2. At their dorm.

3. In a library study room.

4. In a small classroom.

5. In a large lecture hall.

6. In a professor's office.

7. In a teacher assistant's office.

8. On a campus bench.

9. Under a campus tree.

10. In a bathroom.

11. Under the bleachers at the stadium.

12. On the bleachers at the stadium.

13. In a campus parking lot.

14. At the campus gym.

15. In the back row of the campus theater.

16. In a basement.

17. In a locker room.

18. In a campus common area.

19. In the dining hall.

20. In a hallway.

21. On a campus roof.

22. In an administration building.

23. On the football field.

24. In a concessions stand.

25. On the racetrack.

26. On a campus lawn.

27. On a campus shuttle bus.

28. In an elevator.

29. In a fraternity/sorority house.

30. In the communal showers.

31. On the top floor of the tallest building on campus.

44

DO THE WALK OF SHAME*

Dating in college is a little bit of an oxymoron. Times have changed, and it's not exactly what your parents experienced, when many men and women married their college sweethearts.

These days, and we're sure you've seen the obnoxious headlines, college dating is hookup central.

It is rather uncommon to hear two people say they are dating. Instead, they are "hanging out." It makes a lady feel real special. (Note: That was sarcasm.)

That said, if you do find yourself standing in line for popcorn and soda at the local movie theater on a real grown-up date, you've found yourself a good one. Hold onto them.

A typical college date is going over to his/her place to Netflix and chill. It is as romantic as it sounds. If the invite comes through after a certain time (10 p.m.), the emphasis will be on the chill and less so on the Netflix.

---

* Also known as the Stride of Pride.

Other common college hookups will start by meeting someone at a party or in a bar. You'll flirt. You'll have some drinks. You may kiss. And you both decide you want to continue your night together somewhere else. Either their place or yours, but it needs to be consensual. You both are in the right mind to say yes, this is what you want, and off you go for a night of wild and crazy sex.

Which brings us to the walk home in the morning. Sometimes you get lucky (no pun intended), and you're able to bring your hookup buddy back to your place. In which case, they are doing the walk of shame. Sometimes, you'd rather go to their place not thinking about the joyful walk awaiting you in the morning (or afternoon) light. At some point in college, you will be on either ends of the infamous stroll. Naturally, there are a few rules to know and use so that you don't look like a total asshat.

RULES OF THE WALK OF SHAME

1. One must offer any item of clothing to help their guest cover up last night's scantily clad outfit. Especially if it's Halloween weekend.

2. One must offer a ride home if you have a car available.

3. One must offer breakfast.

4. One must offer a shower.

5. One must casually acknowledge the fun that was had.

45

BUY A STRANGER
A DRINK

You spot someone attractive from across the bar. You want to start up a conversation and see if there's a spark between you. Rather than blow your chances with a ridiculous pickup line, you know that offering a free drink is a nice, nonthreatening way to begin getting to know someone.

First, one major rule before you make your move: Wait until the person's current drink is almost gone. While we all love to double fist drinks every now and then, other times it's awkward. It makes you look like an alcoholic, and depending on the drink, it could be getting watered down as the ice melts.

15 WAYS YOU CAN BUY SOMEONE A DRINK

1. Ask the bartender what this person is drinking, then have the bartender make another for you to give.

2. Order two shots and take both over to him/her for you to take together.

3. Order your favorite drink and bring it over.

4. Order a shot, and ask the bartender to deliver it for you.

5. Simply walk over and ask if you can buy him/her a drink.

6. Watching the big game? Make a bet on which team wins— loser buys the winner a drink.

7. Have a friend be your wingman as you approach the cutie in question.

8. Drinking beer? Order a pitcher and offer him/her a glass. After all, sharing is caring.

9. Make eye contact and do an air "cheers." If he/she doesn't approach you, they might not be single.

10. Challenge him/her to a bar game, like darts or billiards. Make a bet that the loser has to buy the winner a drink.

11. Wait until he/she needs another drink, and meet him/her at the bar. Before he/she has a chance to pay, tell him/her that this one is on you.

12. Wait until he/she needs a drink, and make sure you eavesdrop on his/her order. If the drink of choice sounds good to you, tell the bartender to make it two and pick up the tab for both drinks.

13. Be fiscally responsible by starting a conversation before you buy the drink. You don't want to waste your money on someone you don't end up liking!

14. Order a round of shots for your group of friends, and offer him/her to get in on the fun.

15. Forget the drink and just say, "Hi!"

46

SURPRISE YOUR PARENTS BY COMING HOME ON A WEEKEND

Remember your high school days when all your parents did was embarrass you? Well, here's a big revelation for you: your parents are actually pretty cool. We don't personally know them, but based on all the parents we've met, we can safely say they are cooler than you realize. It just takes time to get there. Now that you're in college and becoming a real adult, you will be able to see your relationship change from parent-child to parent-friend.

Once you're old enough and mature enough, your parents will be happy to pop open that bottle of wine and give you a glass. Sometimes, they'll even do this when you're 20. We know, it's shocking. When they see that their job parenting you is pretty much done, they'll relax. And, eventually, they'll tell you about their wild and crazy days when they were your age. Prepare yourself for the unexpected. Your parents lived a whole other life before they had you.

So, the point is, as you grow up, your relationship to your parents will change. They miss you so much. That's why a surprise visit is the best gift you could give them. They know the time you'll spend at their house is limited. You'll come home for holidays, maybe even the whole summer in between school years. But, eventually, you won't come home for the summer. And you may stop coming home for certain holidays. You'll learn about the joy of "friends-giving" (see "Spend Thanksgiving (or any Holiday) with Your Friends" on page 231), and maybe you'll celebrate with your pals when you just can't afford the trip home. Your parents are facing the realization that their time with you is now so very limited. To them, you're going to school today and tomorrow you could be married with a kid on the way. That is how fast time feels to them. And when you are their age, you'll understand. Because it will mean the world to you when your kids surprise you for a weekend at home.

If your school is too far away for a weekend trip, try to surprise your parents by coming home a day or two early for big holiday breaks instead. Those extra days will be treasured forever.

47

SEND A FRIEND A CARE PACKAGE

A hard thing to balance in college is old friends and new friends. You'll try to have phone or Skype dates with your high school friends who went off to other colleges, but eventually, they'll be spaced further and further apart due to your ever-growing social lives. When you meet up at home during school breaks, you may feel like your friendships have picked up right where they left off. But you have, in fact, changed in the time you've spent apart. In order to keep your friendships strong through the years (and inevitable changes) to come, you'll have to realize that these relationships will have their own highs and lows. It is inevitable and it is a normal part of growing up.

When you are missing one of your high school friends, let him/her know you are thinking of them by sending them a care package. If they love it, they'll return the favor. And you can keep your relationship strong with regular packages back and forth. Here are a few themed packages you can put together and mail to your friends:

MOVIE CARE PACKAGE

❑ 2–4 Blu-rays

❑ Box of popcorn

❑ Popcorn seasonings

❑ Red Vines or Twizzlers

❑ M&Ms

❑ Boxes of other candy (e.g., Jujyfruits, Skittles, Starburst, Junior Mints, Butterfinger Bites, Gobstoppers, Sour Patch Kids, Dots, Milk Duds, Mike & Ike, etc.)

❑ Cans of soda

❑ Gift card to a movie theater

SPA CARE PACKAGE

(Send before finals week!)

❑ Hand, foot, and body lotions

❑ Nail polish

❑ Bubble bath

❑ Candle

❑ Eye mask

❑ Facial sheet masks

❑ Loofah

COMFORT FOOD CARE PACKAGE

(Send when your friend is feeling homesick.)

❑ All his/her favorite foods

❑ Chips

❑ Popcorn

❑ Candy and chocolate

❑ Cheesy crackers (Cheez-Its, Goldfish)

- ❑ Boxed macaroni and cheese
- ❑ Any special foods from your hometown
- ❑ Pizza gift card
- ❑ Gum
- ❑ Mints
- ❑ Crackers and squeeze cheese
- ❑ Ice cream gift card

48

TAKE CLASSES THAT ARE OUTSIDE OF YOUR MAJOR

Yes, getting your degree should help prepare for you for a future career. However, taking a whole bunch of business or engineering classes can wear you out. That's why it's important to add in a couple of electives that are for pure pleasure. We're not talking Easy A classes, but rather, a topic in which you are truly interested and would like to expand your knowledge. We've researched real classes available at universities around the country that might not fall into your particular major, but will certainly capture your interest for a semester.

INTRO TO WINES (CALIFORNIA STATE UNIVERSITY, CHICO): This class covers grape growing and winemaking in California wine regions, matching wine and food, and sensory evaluation.

POLITICIZING BEYONCÉ (RUTGERS UNIVERSITY): This class uses Queen Bey's music to explore race, gender, and sexuality in America.

SURVIVING THE COMING ZOMBIE APOCALYPSE (MICHIGAN STATE UNIVERSITY): This online class assigns students to groups to "face multiple challenges and tasks as they attempt to survive the catastrophic event, escape death, and preserve the future of civilization."

ICE CREAM SHORT COURSE (PENNSYLVANIA STATE UNIVERSITY): Instructors take students from "cow to cone" in this annual class. The roster of graduates is a Who's Who of Ice Cream. Participants previously enrolled in this class represent Ben & Jerry's, Baskin-Robbins, Friendly's, Häagen-Dazs, and many others.

#SELFIECLASS (UNIVERSITY OF SOUTHERN CALIFORNIA): Also known as "Writing 150: Writing and Critical Reasoning: Identity and Diversity," this class's freshman students examine "society's influence on self-identity and how selfies reflect and affect the global culture in which we live."

NIP, TUCK, PERM, PIERCE, TATTOO, EMBALM—ADVENTURES WITH EMBODIED CULTURE (ALFRED UNIVERSITY): Freedom of expression is the focus of this class that examines how people modify their bodies.

JAY Z AND KANYE WEST (UNIVERSITY OF MISSOURI, COLUMBIA): Beyoncé isn't the only lecture subject! This class examines how Jay Z and Kayne are similar and different from poets.

49

DITCH A CLASS FOR SOMETHING MORE FUN*

A word to the wise: most professors don't take attendance. So long to the days of saying "Here" when Mr. Jones says your name during roll call. While some professors do acknowledge your presence in order to include participation into your final grade, it is okay to skip a class every now and then. Whether you are glued to your bed with the flu or you're just not in the mood to sit and listen to a lecture, you have the freedom and responsibility to choose to go to class. While Ds get degrees, do not let that be your motto. You don't want to disappoint your parents, now, do you?

So you really should try to make it to all of your classes. When you go to class, you'll learn what will be on midterms and finals. And that alone ups the odds of passing. Yes, college really is that simple.

During the first session of each class, you'll receive a syllabus. That syllabus will tell you the exact days of

* Except on test days. Don't skip those.

important due dates and exam dates. You can also use the syllabus to figure out when nothing that important will happen. If it looks like a Wednesday class will be spent watching a movie, you might want to think about heading to the nearest beach, lake, or mountain (depending on the season) for a day of adventure. And if it looks like a class on Friday is worth skipping, you may realize you can start your weekend getaway on Thursday night instead. (See page 30 for camping tips.)

And don't fret about missing the notes from Prof's lecture. With each college course, you'll make friends. You'll find people to create a study group with. And you'll always have a buddy from whom you can copy their notes.

THINGS THAT ARE GOOD FOR YOUR HEALTH

Fitness schmitness, amirite? College was made for left-over pizza breakfasts, 2 a.m. meals, and endless movie marathons. No one likes a gym rat.

However, taking care of your mental health is just as important as taking care of your physical health. And this chapter covers a few simple tips and tricks you should add to your routine, like, yesterday.

According to some studies, when you adopt healthy habits in these formative years, you are more likely to hold onto them through adulthood. Future you will be so thankful that 20-year-old you did care about going for a weekly run or enjoyed getting into downward dog in the morning.

At first, you'll need to be conscious of your healthy and unhealthy habits. But after some time making healthy choices, they'll start to become second nature. And don't worry—you're still allowed to eat as much pizza as you want; just make sure you also eat some fruit too.

50

SET UP A FITNESS ROUTINE

Being away from home for the first time means figuring out a routine that works for your new life. We don't just mean studying, working, and partying either. It is a good idea to set up good habits that will hopefully stick with you even after you graduate. One of the biggest things you can do for your mental and physical health is regular exercise.

The best resource available to you is your campus gym. Nearly every campus will have some kind of athletic facility, and you would be wise to get to know what it offers. Let's face it, college is expensive enough without shelling out for a costly gym membership. Even better, find out what classes are being offered; that way you can get exercise and college credits at the same time! The options are endless, from dance classes to swimming, weightlifting, or yoga.

For a totally free workout, take up running or get a group of friends together for impromptu soccer or basketball games. Go on hikes on the weekends to get some nature time and help boost your cardio. Do you drive or take public transportation to school? Consider walking or biking for your commute; not only will you increase your daily steps, you will also be saving money (either on gas or bus fares).

Besides the health benefits, regular exercise will also boost your confidence, help you blow off steam from all the studying, and give you opportunities to make friends, especially if you take classes or join a sports team.

Not only will you be taking steps to stay healthy, you will also combat the dreaded weight gain that can creep on after too many nights of boozing and midnight pizza runs. Oh, you can still indulge, but now you can feel like you earned that last beer or slice.

BE SAFETY SMART

So far in this book we've been encouraging you to get out there, make memories, and take risks. But being "safety smart" is a good habit to cultivate for the rest of your life and is especially necessary during your college years!

It's an unfortunate fact of life that college students can be seen as an easy target to a lot of criminals. You're usually away from home for the first time and have expensive computers and other tempting gadgets to steal. Not to mention drinking and partying are staples of college life, which can definitely lead to unsafe situations. These safety tips are for guys as well as gals, so give them a look and stay safe out there!

1. "Buddy up" when walking around at night. No matter how safe your neighborhood is, or if you're a big guy or a petite gal, this is a good safety habit to always remember.

2. Put emergency numbers into your cell phone. If your wallet gets stolen, you want to be able to call your bank and credit cards and cancel any cards that were in there.

3. Always lock your doors and windows. This is an easy one to forget, especially living with roommates that come and go, or in the dorms. But it only takes one distracted moment for someone to sneak in and steal your shit.

4. Put a locking device on your laptop.

5. Use the campus escort service at night. Every campus should have some sort of program for you to call. Say you're leaving the library at night and don't have a buddy to walk you to your car. Call the escort service and someone will be there to assist you.

6. Keep track of your friends when going out. Don't all scatter when you leave the party or the bars, assuming everyone will make it home okay. Check in with each other and even have a designated meet-up spot if you do get separated.

7. Consider taking a self defense class. Not only will it increase your confidence and coordination, but you just might find a physical activity you love and stick with it. On page 127, we discuss finding a fitness routine. Well, you just might find that karate or tae kwon do class fits the bill for fitness and self defense. Win win!

CHANGE UP YOUR DIET

When you're living at home, odds are that you follow a similar diet as the rest of your family. They're the ones providing the food for the most part, so you don't have that much of a say in your day-to-day meals. All that changes when you move out and have to plan your daily meal routine on your own, which opens you up to a world of possibilities!

We'll talk about learning how to master simple recipes in a couple pages, but have you considered exploring a completely new diet? Maybe you want to start cutting animal products out of your diet and want to give veganism a try. Or perhaps you want to see if cutting out gluten will help give you more energy. Now is the time to try out a few different plans and see what feels right to you.

A few things to consider:

1. Be leery of diet plans that require you to buy expensive shakes and supplements. Usually this is for weight loss or muscle-building plans. Most of them don't do half the things they promise and the only weight you will lose will be in your wallet.

2. Consider taking a nutrition class or consulting with a nutritionist at the student health center to figure out more about your individual needs. Often, nutritional majors will offer their services free to earn credits—take advantage!

3. If you're experimenting with a new diet plan, use it as an opportunity to explore new restaurants, or even to order dishes off of familiar menus that you've never tried. At the very least you will expand your palate and gain a new appreciation for different types of cuisine.

4. Talk to your doctor before embarking on any extreme changes in your diet.

5. No matter what diet plan you decide to explore, remember to eat plenty of fruit and veggies!

53

HAVE A RECOVERY DAY

There comes a time in every college student's life when all the partying, studying, working, and just plain living catches up to you. You know what you need? A good old-fashioned recovery day.

Ditch all your classes on a random weekday. This isn't high school anymore, no chance of getting detention for ditching or your parents being pissed. You're an adult now, and you've made an executive decision: time for some well-earned Me Time. Why a weekday? Simple: your roommates will most likely be at school themselves (chumps!) so you will have a full day of uninterrupted quiet time alone. So go ahead: unplug the alarm, put your phone on silent, and sleep as late as you can.

We're not kidding, sleep as late as humanly possible. You don't have to be anywhere, revel in it! When you finally do get up, stay in your pj's. Take a shower if you want, but get right back into those comfy clothes. Make something simple and tasty, or even better, order pizza. Then plop right back into bed or on the couch and have a TV marathon. Paint your nails. Look up some mindless websites, or play a video game. The only rules are no homework or chores or anything productive! This is unscheduled slack time, and it happens all too rarely in our hectic college lives. So savor it!

We guarantee, the next day you will wake up refreshed and recharged. Ready to jump back into the life of tests, studying, keg stands, and all that college has to offer. Just don't make a habit of doing it, even though you don't have to worry about detention You are paying to be there, after all.

LEARN TO COOK

Trust us, you will miss your parents' cooking. After months of eating at the same cafeteria or select few on-campus restaurants, you'll be drooling for real, fresh meals straight from Mom and Dad's stove.

Going away to college is the longest time you will be away from your parents' house. During the days under their roof, you may have cooked a meal for yourself here and there. But going to college and planning three meals a day, every day of the week, is not a simple task.

Once you are living in an apartment with a kitchen of your own, take some time to experiment with food. (Fact: Being a good cook is a great quality to have when it comes to dating.)

To get you started, here are a few signature dishes that everyone should know.

MEDIUM RARE STEAK

Steak (about 1½ inches thick)
Oil
Kosher salt and black pepper

1. Bring steak to room temperature.

2. Adjust racks so the steak will be about 3 inches from the heat source. Turn oven to broil.

3. Lightly coat steak with oil. Then, season with salt and pepper on both sides.

4. When the broiler is hot (about 5 minutes), place the steak under the broiler for 5 minutes on one side. Keep the oven door slightly ajar, so the broiler doesn't overheat and turn off.

5. Flip the steak and cook for 2 minutes.

6. Remove from the oven and place the steak on a plate. Cover it loosely with foil to rest at least 5 minutes before serving.

7. For a medium-well steak, add a minute to each side of cooking.

THE BEST ASPARAGUS

1 bunch thin asparagus spears, trimmed
3 tablespoons olive oil
1½ tablespoons grated Parmesan cheese
1 clove garlic, minced
1 teaspoon sea salt
½ teaspoon ground black pepper
1 tablespoon lemon juice

1. Break off the woody ends of the asparagus by grabbing a stalk at either end and bending until it snaps. It will break where it gets tough.

2. Preheat oven to 425°F.

3. Place asparagus in a large mixing bowl. Drizzle with olive oil and toss to coat. Add Parmesan cheese, garlic, salt, and pepper. Mix again.

4. In a single layer, arrange asparagus onto a baking sheet.

5. Bake until just tender, about 12 to 15 minutes depending on thickness. Sprinkle with lemon juice before serving.

LASAGNA

Literally follow the steps on a box of no-cook lasagna noodles. Feeling creative? Add some layers of zucchini and mushrooms.

THINGS NOT TO TELL MOM OR GRANDMA

A ROUND OF SHOTS FOR EVERYONE! Just kidding.

As you may have guessed, you've made it to the drinking chapter. From inventing your own signature drink to becoming a Beer Pong champion, this chapter provides all of our best drinking advice.

So of course, here is where we need to put a little disclaimer about the dangers of alcohol. First and foremost, please drink responsibly. Yes, underage drinking happens in college. Watch out for your friends just as you hope they will watch out for you. Binge drinking is incredibly prevalent among college students. Learn your limits and learn when to say no to that third, fourth, or fifth shot. Hangovers are nature's reminder that you drank too much. So in short, always, always drink Blue Dolphins (aka water) in between each alcoholic drink. Okay, lecture over.

Flip the page, start reading, drink responsibly, and we promise you you'll graduate college with two degrees: one for your major, and one for socializing.

55

DAY DRINK

Picture this: You wake up on a weekend morning with nothing to do but hang with your friends and take some much-needed chill time. Or there is a daytime event happening, like Super Bowl Sunday or a favorite TV show marathon. What better time to pour a drink, declare it a no study day, and day drink with your friends?

The feeling of getting a nice buzz on while kicking it with friends, listening to music, or watching movies while the sun is still out is something everyone should experience at least once or twice in their college careers. Here are some tips to make it a great and safe time:

1. Drink water! This is the golden rule any time you are tying one on, but something to remember in your day drinking quest, especially if the weather is hot. Alcohol dehydrates you, so be sure and replenish your fluids throughout the day.

2. Day drinking is a marathon, not a sprint! Now is not the time for shots or power hour shenanigans. No, you wanna keep that buzz going all day without getting sloppy and pukey, or worse, passing out and causing your friends to have to rally and take

care of you. Think session beers (beers specially made with lower alcohol), wine spritzers or mimosas, or mixed drinks heavy on the mixers.

So call your friends and neighbors, set up the kiddie pool or sprinkler in the front yard, and declare it day drinking time! Or, if it's a rainy/snowy day outside, have everyone bundle up and start drinking the spiked cocoa (try it with peppermint schnapps, super yummy)! Bonus to day drinking: you probably won't be making it a super-late night, so by the time you're ready to go to bed, you will have plenty of hours to catch up on your beauty sleep and face another week!

56

INVENT A SIGNATURE DRINK

Bored with beers? Vodka tonics making you yawn? Maybe it's time to change up your drinking game, by which we mean invent something else entirely! That's right, it's time you invented a new drink, one which will be remembered throughout the ages at watering holes around the globe! Or it will become a private joke with your friends and great nostalgic reminder of your college years.

There aren't really any hard and fast rules to making your own signature cocktail. But the trick to making a really good, really memorable one is this: have a purpose. Now, this means have a reason behind inventing a new drink. Don't just haphazardly mix gin and vodka together, stick a straw in it, and say "Okay, this drink is called the... (looks around room)...Roommate's Dirty Dishes." Lame! How about the night when your friend Dave got drunk and crawled onto the roof and couldn't get down? What better way to always remember that night than with a Dave's Folly, a cocktail of your own choosing.

A few more pointers:

1. Start by building on established recipes. Try swapping out one liquor for another in a recipe you already know. For example, swap out vodka for gin in a cosmopolitan.

2. Remember to balance the ratio of spirits to mixers; don't make it too weak but also don't tip too heavily in the other direction. Unless you want to end up like Dave.

3. Consider using fresh, in-season ingredients like herbs or fruit you can find at the local farmer's market.

4. Don't forget the garnish! Be creative, it will add an extra note of personality to your drink.

Whatever you come up with, it will be sure to be an instant reminder of your drunken college shenanigans that will make you smile years from now. You can whip up your signature drink and raise a toast to the friends you made and adventures you got into during your crazy college years. Bottoms up!

57

BEFORE YOUR 21ST: TRAVEL TO WHERE YOU CAN DRINK LEGALLY

So you're at college feeling grown up as hell. There's one more milestone that can seem like an unbearably long wait: turning 21. To ease the wait, we recommend using your vacation time to travel to a more accepting country for some underage imbibing!

Some places to consider:

MEXICO

One of the most popular destinations for college students is Mexico, both for the ease of travel (cheap flights are relatively easy to find) and the endless beaches and fun resort towns. Oh yeah, and the plentiful options for some underage margarita guzzling! A lot of these places have all-inclusive packages with airfare, hotel, and sometimes even food and drinks included, so do your homework and make sure you're getting the best deal. Top destinations:

- Cancun
- Puerto Vallarta
- Cabo San Lucas
- Playa Del Carmen

CARIBBEAN

There is no shortage to the amazing places in the Caribbean islands to visit for your spring break adventure. They can range from sleepy seaside villages to all-inclusive resorts that are geared toward the partying twenty-somethings. Check out the different Caribbean destinations and see if it sounds like a good option for you and your pals. Top destinations:

- Jamaica
- Puerto Rico
- Aruba
- Bahamas
- St. Barts
- Barbados

CANADA

If the thought of drunk crowds of woo girls and frat guys on the beach makes you cringe, why not consider our friendly neighbor to the north? The drinking age is 19, the scenery is amazing, and there's always a new adventure to try. Bonus: no need to worry about learning a foreign language to get by (unless you feel like practicing those French skills).

Whether you're hitting up the slopes over winter break or exploring the gorgeous cities during spring or summer, Canada has got you covered for that international travel experience you're craving without getting too far out of your comfort zone. If you are on the East Coast, check out Toronto, Ottawa, or Montreal. If you go to school on the West Coast, consider Vancouver, Calgary, or Victoria.

EUROPE

This may require more planning ahead and saving money, but it's definitely worth it. Whether downing pints with local soccer (sorry, football) hooligans at a pub in England or sipping wine in a piazza in Rome, Europe is a perfect getaway for the adventure-seeking college student. And no, you don't need a ton of time or money to do a European jaunt, just some savvy planning. Shop ahead for airfare (set an alert on airfare aggregator sites like Kayak to alert you for cheap deals), stay in hostels or Airbnb rentals, and do your research on the best deals in whatever city you visit.

58

FIND YOUR OWN CHEERS

What are the benefits to having a local pub that you claim as your own? Glad you asked. Aside from the occasional perks of a free drink and quick service, it's nice to have a place you feel comfortable dropping in at any time. Whether you want a chill place to study or a place to bring a group of friends, claiming a bar as your own is a great way to add to your college experience (and beyond).

Here are some handy tips on how to be a memorable and welcome guest at your new hangout spot.

1. **DO** tip well. Don't feel like you have to empty your wallet for every drink you buy, but for the first order or two, be sure to add a couple extra bucks to your normal tip. You will be remembered fondly.

2. **DON'T** hit on the bartender/staff. Remember, it's their job to be friendly to the customers. Don't mistake it for an invitation.

3. **DO** learn the names of the staff. Greeting people by name is one of the fastest ways to establish a rapport, and in turn, they will most likely remember your name as well.

4. **DON'T** get sloppy. It's a mathematical certainty: get wasted just once to the point when people have to clean up your puke/call a cab and you will forever be known as "that guy/gal."

5. **DO** order wisely. Basically, if the bar is packed and the staff is struggling to keep up, do not be a jag and order something complicated or confusing. Save the flaming daiquiri request for a slower time.

6. **DON'T** bring your obnoxious friends. Everyone has that one friend who can be a bit of a handful when they go out. Whether it's getting crazy, picking fights, or trying to dance on the bar, it's probably a good idea to take them to the club down the street rather than inflicting them on your regular bar and its staff.

7. **DO** come during off-peak hours. This is the perfect way for the staff to get to know your face and for you to be remembered, instead of being one of a sea of faces on a busy Friday night.

Wherever you find to make your regular spot, it will play a large part in creating memories that will last a lifetime. Sure, some of them may be fuzzy, but they will be remembered fondly. Raise a glass!

59

PARTY AT A DIFFERENT COLLEGE

Spending weekends with the same friends at the same bars or parties and talking about the same classes week after week can get really tired. Why not mix it up and party at a totally different school for a night or a whole weekend? Maybe there's another school in the next town over, or even in your own city, that your friends attend or you're just curious about. Or maybe you miss your high school best friend and they go to college in another state, or another country. Go stay in their dorm and let them be your tour guide! You'll get the thrill of being a tourist and see how another campus measures up to yours.

Of course, one of the best ways to check out a different school is to attend some parties. Meet some cool new friends, or even hook up with someone, with the added perk of not having to awkwardly run into them in the hallway or classroom later that week.

Bonus points if you party with people at a school totally different from yours. Is your campus in a small hick town? Go visit one in a big city! Is your school notorious for its wild parties? Try visiting somewhere totally different and find out what they do for fun, whether it's an art school, culinary academy, or even a religious college. You'll expand your mind, make new friends, and probably appreciate your campus even more when you return.

Or, maybe you'll fall in love with another campus. It is totally okay to switch schools the following semester or year if you felt like another school is more compatible to you. Of course, do your research first to make sure they offer courses in the major you want to pursue and that your credits will transfer, and find out about any financial issues that come up. The first college you go to does not necessarily have to be the one you graduate from.

60

PREGAME BEFORE GOING OUT

A drinking financial lesson for you: the more you drink for free at home before going out, the less money you will spend on drinks once you are out.

After turning 21, it is wise to invest in a stock of booze for your apartment to imbibe before a night out at the bars.

What should you keep on hand? Depends on your preference, but it's good to have a variety of spirits to offer when you have friends over. The staples are gin, vodka, rum, and tequila. You may want to keep a couple different types of beer on hand. And if you are a wino, have both red and white varietals in stock as well.

If you plan to keep your spirits stocked, you'll also need mixers and chasers. For gin, many prefer tonic water. Vodka can go with pretty much anything. Rum goes well with soda or juices. Tequila also pairs well with juice, though you'll want to keep limes on hand if you plan to take tequila shots.

To successfully pregame is an art. One needs to be able to know their limit and not exceed that before even leaving the confines of their own home.

It's wise to stay between two or three drinks, though that will vary depending on your tolerance. And though we'll sound like a mom right now, don't forget to drink some water every now and then. You will have more drinks once you hit the bars, and it's responsible to pace yourself.

Now that we got the drinks covered, what else should you know about pregaming? Well, it's often the most fun part of your night! To plan a killer pregame hang, make sure your friends arrive an hour or two before you plan to go out. That will give you all plenty of time to get ready together, blast some tunes, and have some drinks. Throw in some time to take selfies and you'll almost forget why you even want to go out when you're having so much fun staying in.

61

MEMORIZE THE NIGHTLY DRINK SPECIALS AROUND TOWN

It may sound shocking, but a local weekly newspaper in our college town actually printed all the town's drink specials in every issue. It was brilliant. Naturally, it saved the students from having to do the research themselves, and it helped the bars with free advertising.

The best thing about college bars is that they know their clientele. They know students don't have six figure salaries to pay for bottle service or $15 martinis. They know it's better to pack in the students with crazy cheap deals and make their money through quantity. (Because college students drink a lot.)

From power hours and buck nights to ladies' night and Sunday Funday specials, the bars around your campus will have some sort of drinking special every night of the week.

If you don't have a source for all that information, make your own calendar. Do the research to find what nights have the best deals. Check out the bars' Facebook, Twitter, or Instagram pages as they may list their specials there. You can save the info in your iPhone's notes or calendar apps. Or you can create a Google calendar to share with your friends so you can all plan where you will go. We have the days of the week listed here for you to take notes and share with your friends.

DAY	BAR SPECIAL
Sunday	
Monday	
Tuesday	
Wednesday	
Thursday	
Friday	
Saturday	

62

DISCOVER THE BEST MEALS AT 2 A.M.

It is a universal truth that nothing tastes as good as hot, fresh pizza at 2 o'clock in the morning after a night of drinking.

When the bars close, you'll see many people stumbling home. Those people are clueless, so forget them. When the bars close, you should be in search of food instead of going home. Also, it will help minimize the hangover, so there's that.

From scouting 24-hour diners and late-night pizza to discovering an authentic taco truck and hole-in-the-wall places that serve the best food, it is your job to find the best 2 a.m. meals.

It's going to take some time, but once you find your top picks, you won't regret it. You might have some epic fails and bad meals, but you will also find the best burger of your life.

The late night (or early morning) meals will be unforgettable memories for you and your friends. As you're downing a slice of pizza or shoving your face into a plate of nachos, you'll be capping the night off in the best way—hanging out with your favorite people.

Depending on how much alcohol was previously consumed, you may not remember the conversations you'll have. But these will be some of the best talks of your life. The conversations will be deep. You'll recap the events of the night, reliving the most hysterical moments. But you might also get philosophical about your future and where you want your life to go. Or, if you're the drunkest one that particular night, you may make a fool of yourself, but who cares? You're young and you're living it up!

These are the moments that make college the best years of your life.

63

DANCE ON A BAR

Time to take things Coyote Ugly!

For all the ladies, dancing on a bar is a rite of passage. Just like riding a mechanical bull. It is a chance to own your sexuality without judgment. In that moment, you must be 100 percent carefree. All that matters is dancing.

Before you embark on this bucket list item, you must know which bar will allow you to dance on it. Unfortunately, for many bars, it is a liability to have anyone dance on a bar. For obvious reasons (injury), of course. So it may take some research to figure out where you can pull it off.

Next, once the location is secured, you need to reach the right level of being buzzed. You can't be too drunk because your dance moves will be awful. You can't be too sober because you won't have the courage to really get into it. There is a perfect level where you are just drunk enough to let your hair down and sober enough to keep your balance.

Then, you need to pick your song. Make sure the bartender or DJ knows your jam before you hop on the bar. When your song plays, it's time to go!

Not sure which tune to pick? We've got you covered.

TOP 15 DANCING-ON-A-BAR SONGS

1. "Pour Some Sugar on Me" by Def Leppard
2. "Livin' on a Prayer" by Bon Jovi
3. "Unbelievable" by EMF
4. "Need You Tonight" by INXS
5. "Single Ladies (Put a Ring on It)" by Beyoncé
6. "Baby Got Back" by Sir Mix-a-Lot
7. "Welcome to the Jungle" by Guns N' Roses
8. "I Want to Dance with Somebody" by Whitney Houston
9. "I Gotta Feeling" by Black Eyed Peas
10. "You Shook Me All Night Long" by AC/DC
11. "OMG" by Usher
12. "Don't Cha" by Pussycat Dolls
13. "Just Dance" by Lady Gaga
14. "Dancing in the Dark" by Bruce Springsteen
15. "Apple Bottom Jeans" by T-Pain

64

LEARN DRINKING TRICKS

Impress your pals with your skills. Learn here the secrets to these drinking tricks so that you don't look like an amateur when everyone is taking turns doing keg stands.

SHOTGUN A BEER

Only drinks in cans can be used for this. To shotgun your drink, you'll puncture a hole in the side of the can, close to the bottom rim. Hold the can horizontally so that the liquid doesn't spill out. You'll then place your mouth over that hole and rotate the can straight up. Lift your head and can at the same time so you are comfortably standing. When you are ready, pull the can's tab open. The drink will quickly drain through the hole into your mouth. Drink as fast as you can! Shotgunning can also be used as a competition.

DO A KEG STAND

A classic frat party event! To do a keg stand, you'll place your hands on the keg's handles. Other people will lift your legs so you're almost in a handstand. Someone else will put the keg tap into your mouth, and they'll control the speed and flow of the beer. You'll try to drink as much as you can upside down. When you are finished, you can take your mouth off the tap and the people holding your legs will put you down. This can also be a drinking contest to see who can do the longest keg stand.

PROPERLY TAKE A SHOT

Pick your poison and pick your chaser. Some people choose to take a sip of their chaser to hold in their mouth before taking the shot. Then, you'll swallow the chaser and the shot at the same time. Once you have swallowed, you can take another sip of the chaser.

To help the shot slide down your throat, you'll tilt your head back as you bring the shot glass to your mouth. Swallow the shot immediately. Holding the alcohol in your mouth will make it harder to swallow as you'll taste how strong it is. Remember to also keep your jaw and throat relaxed and the whole process will be over in an instant.

65

PLAY AND MASTER CLASSIC PARTY DRINKING GAMES

You can't go to a party and not see one of these three epic games being played. Start practicing your Beer Pong bounce now, as you're going to have to use it. If you are good at any of these games (King's Cup takes the least amount of physical skill), you'll definitely be drafted to the best teams. Read and learn the rules now so that when you hit up those college parties, you won't be the player asking for someone to explain how to play. You'll be able to teach others. And that will give you the cool factor.

BEER PONG

PLAYERS: 2–4

MATERIALS:

22 Solo cups (20 for the game, 2 for rinsing the balls)
2 ping-pong balls

Beer

Water

This is, hands down, the most popular college drinking game of all time. It's even international. Study abroad, and you'll likely see your foreign peers playing it as well.

While it is a drinking game, it does actually require some serious hand-eye coordination. Some rules are standard, though there are opportunities to create your own "house rules." If you are playing on someone else's turf, ask about their house rules. It's a rookie mistake to try to challenge house rules.

HOW TO PLAY:

1. Play one on one or in teams of two. With teams of two, players will take turns throwing the ball each time their team gets a turn.

2. Fill 20 cups with beer. To conserve your beer stash, fill up each cup to the first line inside the cup. To drink more in a game, fill up cups halfway with beer. Typically, 3–4 beers are enough for all 20 cups.

3. Fill the 2 extra cups with clean water to rinse balls between throws.

4. Arrange the 10 cups into a triangle (base row of 4, then 3, 2, and 1). The triangle can also be set up with 6 cups if you want faster moving games.

5. Determine which team starts. One player from each team will look at each other eye to eye and throw one ball at the opposing cups. The first player to make a cup will start the game.

6. Take turns throwing the balls into cups. Each player throws one ball. See below for variations on throwing techniques.

7. When a ball goes into a cup, the team on that side of the table must drink the beer. Players alternate drinking the beer. Set the cup aside. Do not stack cups—it's bad luck.

8. As cups get removed, the triangle can be reshaped. When 6 cups remain, form another triangle. When 4 cups remain, create a diamond. When 2 cups remain, file into a single line.

9. Keep playing until one team has no cups remaining. The team who has no cups loses, and the other team wins.

Variations:

• Rather than taking turns following each shot, a player will continue with their turn each time they make a shot.

• Give the losing team a redemption shot. This is called a "rebuttal," where they have one last chance to stay in the game. If they make the ball into one of the opposing teams' cups in their last turn, a 3-cup overtime is started. The teams compete in sudden death to determine the winner.

• A bounce shot counts for 2 cups. If a bounce shot is made, the team must drink 2 cups, one of which is their choosing.

KING'S CUP RULES

PLAYERS: 2+

MATERIALS:

> *1 empty plastic cup*
> *Standard deck of cards*
> *Alcohol of choice (beer, wine, cocktail)*

HOW TO PLAY:

1. Place an empty cup in the center of a table. Remove the jokers from the deck of cards. Spread the deck face down around the cup, forming a circle.

2. Each card has its rules (defined below). Make sure to have this list handy throughout the game—or come up with your own.

3. Players, each with a drink, gather around the table. To start, one player draws a card. The group will then follow the rules of that specific card. Then, the next person draws a card, and players again must participate in the rules of that card, and so on.

4. The game either ends when the last rule card has been pulled, or when the king's cup has been consumed.

ACE: Waterfall. Everyone must drink until the player who drew the card stops drinking. It is up to the player to decide how long to drink.

2: You. Player picks one person to take a drink.

3: Three is me. Player takes a drink.

4: Floor. Everyone must touch the floor. The last player to do so must drink.

5: Dudes. All male players take a drink.

6: Chicks. All female players take a drink.

7: Heaven. Last person to raise their hand must drink.

8: Mates. The player selects another player to drink every time they do. This lasts until someone draws the next eight.

9: Rhymes. The player says a word. Going around the table, each player must say a word that rhymes with it. The player to fail in rhyming has to drink.

10: Categories. The player comes up with a category of things, and each person must come up with something that falls within that category. The player who can't come up with an answer must drink.

JACK: Thumbs. The player will place their thumb on the edge of the table. Try to do this without anyone noticing. As the other players catch on, they too will place their thumbs on the table. The last player to do so will drink.

QUEEN: Wild card. The player will make up a new rule that lasts until the end of the game. Examples: Drink with only your left hand. Don't use first names. Cheers before every drink.

KING: When a player draws a king, they must pour a portion of their drink into the center cup. The player who draws the fourth and final king must drink the entire cup.

FLIP CUP

PLAYERS: 4+

MATERIALS:

> *Red Solo cups (1 cup per player)*
> *Beer (Typically, one can of beer can be used in about three Solo cups.)*

HOW TO PLAY:

1. Form two teams, each with an equal number of players. These teams will stand on opposite sides of a table. The players directly facing each other are opponents. Each person gets a Solo cup filled with a set amount of beer (generally, the second line inside the cup is a marker for how much beer to use).

2. The first two players at one end of the table will start the game with a toast and then drink the entirety of their beer. When finished, they'll place the cup at the edge of the table (open side up), and attempt to flip the cup by flicking or tapping the bottom until it flips and lands upside down on the table (sitting on its mouth). Players must only use one hand to flip the cup. If the cup does not flip, players will reset the cup and try to flip it again. Only after the cup is properly flipped can the next teammate begin to drink their beer. Players cannot touch their cups until the player before them has successfully flipped their cup. And so on down the line until one team has finished all their drinks and flipped all their cups. The first team to do so is the winner.

THINGS THAT ARE A RITE OF PASSAGE

As we said earlier, you are fully in the process of becoming a real-life adult. Cue the frightening screams!

Just as graduation is a rite of passage to the real world, there are many other accomplishments to check off before you finish your degree. The items on the following pages are college staples—they are the experiences you see in the movies, the things that help you feel like you are growing up, and the moments when you feel like you are doing your part in making the world a better place.

As you check each one off the college to-do list, you'll get a taste for adulthood and realize, like we have, that it's actually pretty awesome when your parents stop "parenting" you.

66

COOK DINNER FOR YOUR PARENTS (BONUS: MAKE IT A HOLIDAY DINNER)

Picture this: You're at home from being away at college for the first time. The parents are peppering you with questions about your life, your grades, and on and on. The topic of dinner comes up. "Why don't you let me handle dinner tonight, guys?" you casually announce. Stunned silence. You smile as you rifle through the pantry. "You guys like Italian? Dad, why don't you pop open a bottle of red and let it breathe? It'll complement the main course perfectly." Your parents gape at each other in disbelief. Who is this adult that is now confidently chopping veggies in their kitchen?

Okay, so we're working off the assumption that you did not do a lot of the cooking while living under your parent's roof. Well, why not take this opportunity to show them how far you've come in your ability to take care of yourself and be an adult? It doesn't have to be a gourmet four-course meal, it can be a dish you've mastered that we covered in Learn to Cook on page 135. Combine a simple casserole or main dish with a salad or grilled veggies and your parents will swoon.

Bonus round for the advanced cook: Offer to cook a holiday meal! Or, at the very least, volunteer to be in charge of one or more of the side dishes. This would be a fun way to bond with your parents while you cook a meal together. You may even pick up more cooking tips from them that you can take back with you when you go back to school.

This is also a foolproof way to smooth things over if you're in hot water over your grades or if you're blowing through your monthly budget too fast. It's a good way to say them, "Hey parents, I may have let my grades dip in that one class, and yes I may have blown my monthly budget in the first week on booze, but have you tried my pasta primavera? Adulting success!"

67

BE THE DESIGNATED DRIVER FOR THE NIGHT

Every college student, no matter how often they party, should take at least one turn being the designated driver for the night.

Let's face it, everyone needs to take a night off from partying once in a while, especially if you just want to relax and recharge while your roommates are out on the town. Enjoy having the place to yourself and give your liver a much-needed break. Have them call or text when they're finally ready to come home, then listen in amusement to their drunken rambling stories about all the shenanigans they got into that night. It's a very eye-opening experience to see the end of a weekend night from a sober perspective. You might even think to yourself, "Jeez, do I sound that ridiculous when I come home trashed?" (Answer: yes, yes you do.)

Maybe you don't want to drink, but don't want to have to stay home, either. Then go to the parties and bars along with your friends and see the night out from a unique perspective: the sober one. Think about all the advantages: You can actually have a decent conversation with someone and remember it the next day (maybe they won't, but still). You can chat up that cute guy/girl and sound witty and smart without liquid courage. You will also save lots of money, especially if a bar crawl is on the agenda.

You're probably going to see quite a few people doing very dumb things, like trying to start fights and puking in the gutter. Remember them the next time you are out drinking and resolve to not be "that guy/girl."

Another big advantage: Your friends will owe you, big time. Next night out, it's your turn to get crazy and have one of them be responsible for making sure you get home in one piece.

68

GO SKINNY DIPPING

Skinny dipping is an experience that everyone must do at least once. There is not a better end to a crazy night out with your friends than finding a dark swimming pool and having everyone drop trou and swim around under the stars. Talk about making memories for a lifetime!

Unless you want to end up in the campus newspaper under "Police Blotter," here are some tips to ensure your crazy night doesn't end up in a holding cell down at the police station.

First thing to remember: make sure it's late enough at night so the least amount of people have a chance at stumbling on your bare ass. Secondly, remember to keep your voice down! Now is not the time for cannonballs and yelling at the top of your lungs. If you have trouble remembering this, just picture your parents getting your phone call from jail and having to tell them you're booked on indecent exposure charges. Fun!

The easiest places to take part in some naked night swimming is, of course, the pool at your or your friend's apartment. Stealthy skinny dipping spots include local hotels, gyms, and if you're really ballsy, the pool at your college. Get ready to run if the campus cop sees you though.

If you're thinking, "Woah, this sounds too risky for me," then have we got a suggestion for you. Why not try skinny dipping in the great outdoors? On page 30, we advise you to camp out near a body of water. Well, there's your opportunity! No one around for miles (except your fellow campers) means you definitely don't have to be as stealthy as if you were in a public pool. Keep in mind, though, that just because you don't have to worry about cops doesn't mean there aren't some drawbacks. Two words: water snakes.

69

REGISTER TO VOTE

The best thing about turning 18 is you are now legally able to vote. As you will hear from many people around you, voting is an important responsibility. You should already know that your vote matters. In recent years, voting has helped changed laws around the right to marriage, the legalization of marijuana in many states, higher minimum wages, and so much more.

You may feel like your voice is small and one vote doesn't make a difference. But it does. It really does.

15 REASONS WHY YOU SHOULD VOTE

1. You are voting for more than just the president.

2. You are voting for changes on a local level as well as a national level.

3. Higher voter turnout makes our democracy more representative of the whole picture.

4. Voting is a right that many generations before us fought to win. Women haven't even had the right to vote for 100 years.

5. College students are a big population. There are 44 million of you eligible to vote. Not even 20 percent of 18- to 29-year-olds cast ballots in the 2014 elections, which was the lowest youth turnout rate ever recorded in a federal election.

6. You're in college and you're learning how to voice your opinions. Heck, you are simply just learning what your opinions are. Once you know what you stand for, you can use your vote to support your beliefs.

7. The votes you cast today really make a difference for your tomorrow. Within the next decade, you could have a job, get married, start a family, buy a house, pay for healthcare, or build your own business. The policies and politicians you vote for can have a huge effect on your future.

8. You think college is expensive? Childcare actually costs more. If you think that should change, you should vote.

9. You joke about moving to Canada if a certain someone gets elected as president. If you vote, you can help make your country more like Canada.

10. Politicians pay attention to who votes. If they see they got a big youth vote, they'll pay more attention to youth issues.

11. Your generation is known for creating real change. Millennials are the most open-minded group in terms of social issues.

12. It's easy to register.

13. You get the cool "I Voted!" sticker.

14. It's your right.

15. If you don't vote, you can't complain.

70

VOLUNTEER FOR A POLITICAL CAMPAIGN

Whether you want to lend your support to a local candidate or you want to get involved in the local campaign for a presidential nominee, getting that close to an election and the political process is an invaluable learning experience. Here are the most frequently asked questions about volunteering for a political campaign.

Q: How do you sign up?

A: Find your school's campus democrat or republican clubs. Find out when and where they meet and crash the next one. Once you're there, the opportunities to help on a campaign will come to you. Local candidates will want millennial votes, so they'll be looking for millennials to help get the word out about their platform. If your school doesn't have political clubs, hop on Google to find a candidate you like and want to support, then find their local offices. Stop by when you can and tell them you'd like to volunteer for an hour or so, and they'll be sure to put you on some interesting projects.

Q: What will you do as a volunteer?

A: A little bit of everything really! You may be assigned to speak directly to voters through phone calls or canvassing, where you'll knock on doors, ask questions and collect information, and help register voters. You may be asked to reach out to more of your fellow college students to get them more engaged in the election. You could set up a table on campus to share more information about a specific candidate and his/her policies. Or you may hand out fliers that detail their platform. If you are social media savvy, you can talk to a campaign manager about your skills and how you can help the campaign. You'll get to see the inner workings of a campaign that many people don't!

Q: Why should you volunteer?

A: As stated above, it's an opportunity to get as close to a campaign as you can without being the actual candidate. You'll get a better understanding of how our government works. You'll have a deeper appreciation for the democratic process. You'll see how real change can happen. Plus, you can make your own hours. If you only want to work one hour a week, you are able to do that. If you want to help more, they'll take your services. In any campaign, there is always something more that can be done. You will help make that happen. When the campaign is over, you will feel a sense of accomplishment for all the hard work you put into it.

71

PULL AN ALL-NIGHTER

Ask any college student ever, and the answer will always be, "Yes, I have definitely pulled an all-nighter." We personally do our best writing when we feel the pressure of a deadline, which means at the last minute. Many of our own college papers were done the night before they were due, and one of us never got below a B+. (Not that we're encouraging slacker behavior, but in college, you'll discover when and where you do your best work.)

So unless you are that one person who has never procrastinated once in his/her life, it is inevitable that (at least once) you will stay up all night either cramming for a test, typing as fast as you can to finish that 10-page essay, or finishing a group project because your group totally bailed on you.

There are a few secrets to making your all-nighter more effective. It is not simply to study, type, or read all night 'til the morning hours, then head to class without any sleep. You can actually pull an all-nighter and still get a couple hours of sleep! It's true. Studies prove that sleeping after studying will help you retain the information.

7 STEPS TO GETTING AN A AFTER AN ALL-NIGHTER

1. Bank on sleep before the all-nighter. As soon as you know you'll need to pull an all-nighter, start getting a little more sleep leading up to it. You can also take a nap prior to starting your all-nighter. Do not nap in the middle, because if you are too tired, you might not wake up for hours. Experts say a 60-minute nap is best for remembering facts, places, and faces (good for studying); the downside is that you may have some grogginess when you wake up.

2. Snacks. Avoid carbs. Eat protein. While you may want those potato chips or pizza, skip them. Carbs will store your energy for later and could make you more drowsy. Proteins will keep your energy levels up throughout the night. Go for beef jerky, yogurt and berries, or an apple and peanut butter.

3. Be smart with your caffeine intake. You do not want to OD on caffeine. One to two cups of coffee are perfect for staying focused. Anything more and you risk becoming jittery and losing focus. You can also have an energy drink (though it's not the healthiest option), but be prepared for a big crash later. You also don't want to start on the java train until you really need it. Work hard for a few hours before having your first cup. Then, drink the first cup when you are starting to fade a little.

4. Stay hydrated with water. Every function of your body works better when you are hydrated, including concentration.

5. Chew gum. Some studies have shown that you can increase alertness when chewing gum. Opt for a mint flavor to help increase cerebral activity.

6. Do some exercise. Don't overdo it with a full-body routine, but rather, get your blood flowing with some jumping jacks, lightly jogging in place, or some push-ups.

7. When you're done, get some rest. You made it! You met your deadline and crushed the assignment! Now, it's time to sleep smart. You don't want to throw off your whole system by going to sleep for 8 hours at 8 a.m.. You need to get back to your normal schedule properly. You can allow yourself a short nap, but try to wait until your normal bedtime to crash. Make sure to get a full night's sleep so you wake up feeling refreshed.

72

GO ON A BAR CRAWL

Also known as a pub crawl, a bar crawl is the act of getting a group of people to travel on foot and drink at multiple bars in one night. It's a college staple, and you must participate in at least one bar crawl during your college years. Whoever is organizing it will likely reach out to the bars beforehand to make sure they can accommodate a large group of people all at once. The bar could offer drink specials for your group. You may score a matching T-shirt for your participation, which—win. Who doesn't love a free shirt? (Note: Depending on who is organizing it, there may or may not be a fee to participate and to cover costs of making shirts for everyone.) Another way to do this is instead of walking to each bar, you'll bike. But be careful not to get a BUI. It's a real thing.

A bar crawl is a perfect celebration of any occasion, including but not limited to these:

1. Birthdays

2. Christmas

3. Hanukkah

4. Valentine's Day

5. Easter

6. Spring Break

7. St. Patrick's Day

8. Halloween

9. Thanksgiving

10. New Year's Eve

11. Finals are over.

12. Your friend is single again.

13. Your other friend is single again.

14. You all passed a huge test.

15. You all passed a tough class.

16. A costume bar crawl

17. Pub Golf

18. The Snuggie Bar Crawl

19. Where's Waldo

20. Just because you want to, goddammit.

73

LIVE IN THE DORMS AND LIVE OFF CAMPUS

The college experience wouldn't be complete without living for at least a semester in the dorms, and then finding your own off-campus living arrangement. Both options come with their own set of pros and cons to contend with. Let's explore living in a dorm first.

DORM LIVING

PROS

1. You are living at the epicenter of your campus, with your classes, student center, library, and other on-campus activities within close walking distance. Talk about an easy way to feel immersed in student life!

2. It's nice when you're living away from home for the first time to not have to worry about rent, groceries, or utilities.

3. Your Resident Advisors can help you out and be a support system, should anything come up.

4. Your roommate(s) will totally be on the same page as you when it comes to the stress of college life.

5. Built-in social life! There's almost always someone hanging around to talk to or to go to lunch with.

CONS

1. You almost never get a say in who your roommates will be, so it's a big gamble that you will be compatible and will be able to cohabitate in harmony.

2. That built-in social life? It can also be kind of inescapable. If you're craving alone time or just some quiet study time, it may be a little hard to come by.

3. Shared bathrooms.

4. It's damn near impossible to cook a meal for yourself, so you have to rely on the hours of the cafeteria or takeout food.

OFF-CAMPUS LIVING

Off-campus living comes with its own set of perks and things to deal with.

PROS

1. Privacy! Even if you have roommates, you will most likely have a room all to yourself.

2. You can cook your own food and eat on your schedule, rather than relying on the cafeteria.

3. No adults around to monitor your activities!

4. It can be very nice to get away from campus and have some separation from the craziness of college life.

CONS

1. All the cooking, cleaning, and other household tasks will have to be figured out between you and your roomies.

2. Dealing with rent, utilities, Internet, and other bills can be a hassle to keep track of, as well as a higher expense.

3. All the furniture, decorations, and kitchen supplies can really add up when you first move in.

4. Transportation to and from school needs to be factored in as well.

5. It can feel more isolating being away from the campus, and may be harder on your social life.

74

GO TO A FRAT PARTY

Say goodbye to curfews and hello to warm keg beer! Your college experience isn't complete without inviting yourself to a frat party. If you don't know anyone in a fraternity yet, don't fret. It's really easy. On any given Thursday, Friday, or Saturday night, you must simply walk over to the neighborhood where the frat houses reside. There's bound to be a number of frat guys standing outside looking for fresh faces and future pledges to invite in. Which house you choose is up to you and your friends. There are a few other things you should know before going. You do not want to make any freshman mistakes.

1. **DO** learn the fraternity names. While you might not know the Greek alphabet, you can ask around to find which houses have the best parties. Then, once you're there, make sure you do know the name (or at least the frat's nickname, like Sigma Phi Epsilon goes by Sig Ep). Plus, it can also get confusing when you meet guys who are at one frat's party but belong to a different fraternity.

2. **DON'T** look like a newbie. Leave the school lanyard in your dorm. Keep your keys in your pocket or your purse when you go out.

3. **DO** dress for the theme. Many frat parties will host theme parties (see page 54), and it's always really fun to get into the spirit. If you are going to a theme party, you may want to choose to stay at that party all night rather than party hop. You could look a bit out of place if you walk into a Casino Party having just come from a Pajama Party.

4. **DON'T** go home with anyone without telling your friends first. If you are vibing with someone, make sure to give your friends all the details about where you're going, with whom, and when you'll be back home.

5. **DO** go with friends. Safety in numbers. The buddy system still applies, even in college.

6. **DON'T** challenge the house rules for drinking games. See page 162 for an overview of typical rules for popular drinking games like Beer Pong and Flip Cup. But remember that each house may change the rules to their liking.

7. **DO** stand in smaller groups. Even if you arrived with 10 of your best girlfriends, break up into a couple of smaller groups. The smaller the group, the more comfortable the guys will feel to approach you.

8. **DO** decide if you want to pledge a fraternity. Going to the parties will give you an inside look at the different houses and what the guys are like. You may find one house where you get along with all the guys—and they could be friends for life.

9. **DON'T** stick around if the cops show up. It doesn't happen often, but when the cops arrive, that is your cue to put your drink down and leave—especially if you are underage.

10. **DO** use who you know to your advantage. If a friend of a friend is in the frat, you'll be sure to get VIP treatment. You'll get to skip the lines, a place to store your coat (so it won't get stolen by accident), and maybe a mixed drink of your choice.

11. Ladies, **DON'T** make out with all the frat guys. Only kiss the ones you really like. You don't want to get a bad reputation within a frat. Unfortunately, guys talk and they don't always say the nicest things about women.

12. Guys, **DON'T** make out with any women who are in the same group of friends. Just like you and your pals, ladies talk. You'll lose your chance if you try to pursue more than one romantic interest at a time.

13. **DO** have so much fun! You're at a frat party with your friends and you don't have a curfew. Life is good!

75

MAKE SOME EXTRA CASH

Even if you have financial aid, scholarships, or are lucky enough to have parents footing the bill, there is no getting around the fact that college is expensive. The term "starving student" may be a cliché, but it can also be a reality when you're coming up to the end of the month and only have a few bucks left in your account or dining card, especially if you want to still be able to go out with friends and have a life. It's time to get creative with a side hustle and make some extra paper!

CAMPUS JOBS

The easiest way to make a job work with your already-packed schedule of classes, studying, and social life is to work on campus. Check with the employment office and see what's available that can work around your schedule. Bonus if they're jobs that let you multitask, such as being a secretary in a department that allows you to work on a computer in your downtime. Get paid to get homework done!

CLEAN OUT THE CLOSET

Even if you have a small living space in an apartment or dorm, you inevitably have clothes, shoes, and random stuff you no longer want or use. Or maybe your space is too small to fit that chair or table you thought you'd need. Don't leave it on the curb for someone else to grab, get some bucks for it! Craigslist is great for selling stuff fast, but there are also a number of apps that allow you to quickly snap a pic and sell unwanted clothes and stuff through your phone. Or do you and a group of friends have a bunch of stuff you no longer want? Combine forces and hold a yard sale! You'd be surprised at how quickly the cash can add up, and you get the bonus of being able to declutter your pad.

RANDOM GIGS

There are a ton of ways to earn extra cash through random small jobs found online, such as taking surveys, writing reviews, or doing quick gigs. Websites like Fiverr let you get paid for any odd job you can think of depending on your skillset, including editing a paper, drawing a picture, or writing a song. Apps like TaskRabbit allow you to earn cash doing jobs for people locally, like walking their dog, picking up dry cleaning, or grocery shopping. Little jobs can add up to big money if you do them whenever you have some free time.

Other ideas include tutoring (get paid to keep your knowledge sharp!), babysitting, yard work, event catering, etc. Go out there and make that dough!

THINGS TO
ADD TO YOUR
RESUME

Time to get academic for a minute. College is preparing you to enter the working world. Even before you are handed your degree, you'll be looking and applying for internships or jobs during your final semester or quarter. No time for senioritis when you're trying to avoid moving back in with your parents—although it's totally commonplace to do so. According to a recent survey by the job site Indeed, 36 percent of graduating seniors plan to live at home at least a year or more after graduation.

To sum it up, the sooner you start thinking about your career path, the better. As you'll see on the following pages, the more internships you can put on your resume, the better you'll look as one of a thousand faceless candidates applying for any ol' entry-level job.

Think of college as high school 2.0. In high school, you had to do anything and everything you could to make yourself an attractive prospective student. In college, now you must do the same to make yourself an attractive future employee. Follow our advice, and you may just find yourself with multiple job offers waiting for you.

76

BECOME INVOLVED IN THE SCHOOL PAPER

Unless you're a journalism major, you probably don't give much thought to your school's newspaper beyond flipping through it between classes to kill time; but have you ever thought about what it could do for you? The newspaper is intended to be a voice for students, so why not write a letter to the editor or ask to submit an editorial about an issue you're passionate about? It can be as far-reaching as a major national issue like gun control, immigration, or abortion rights, or as close to home as a campus issue such as the quality of food in the cafeteria or whether you think there should be better lighting and security for students walking home at night. Whatever the issue is that you care about, this is the perfect outlet to get your voice out there, so use it!

Similarly, is there something the newspaper is not covering that you think they should? Could an upcoming concert or theater production you're involved in use some love? Find out who the relevant writer or editor is and reach out to them with the details. Promote whatever event you are involved in and take advantage of the free publicity that the paper offers. They may even ask to interview you. Your parents will be so proud!

You could also try your hand at being directly involved in the paper for a semester just to hone your skills in writing, photography, copy editing, or web design. Even if you don't plan to go into working in media, there's a wealth of knowledge to be gleaned from taking advantage of your campus paper. You would be amazed at how the skills you learn by working on a newspaper can translate to other careers. If nothing else, the skills you acquire will look great on a resume. So check it out!

77

UTILIZE YOUR PROFESSOR'S OFFICE HOURS

Every professor has office hours listed on their door. It would be wise of you to take advantage of them. You may be wondering why. After all, don't you spend enough time in their class? Why would you intentionally want to spend more time with your professors, especially if they're not the friendliest or most interesting? Here are a few reasons:

1. You can ask about any extra credit assignments that are available.

2. You'll learn more about his/her teaching style.

3. In a class of 200+ students, it will help you stand out.

4. It's basically a one-on-one tutoring session.

5. Tough grader? Ask how to improve your grade.

6. Now is your chance to ask that question about the lecture you were too shy to raise your hand about in front of everyone.

7. Is a big project or test coming up? Ask how you can best prepare for it.

Get the picture? Even the professors who seem intimidating are usually much more approachable in a one-on-one situation. So make a point to take advantage of the office hours they provide. You usually have to sign up ahead of time, so be sure to look into that. After all, you're there to get the most of your education. It is totally your right to ask for extra help and time with your professors if it's needed. They will not feel like you're bothering them either; in fact, they will most likely be impressed with your initiative. They have the office hours for a reason after all, might as well use them! College really is what you make of it. You can either coast through and get by doing the bare minimum, or you can really go the extra mile and get the most out of every class.

78

ATTEMPT TO LEARN A DIFFERENT LANGUAGE

Want to broaden your knowledge, immerse yourself in another culture, and become more desirable on your resume? Why not learn a foreign language?

Many jobs today look favorably on hiring people who are bilingual, especially in languages spoken in countries that do a lot of business with the US. A few of the most desirable languages to further your career are:

MANDARIN: One of the most spoken languages in the world, this can open many doors in a ton of careers. It is known as one of the most difficult languages for English speakers to learn, so it will be sure to impress anyone.

SPANISH: This is considered one of the easiest languages to learn and is spoken in over 20 countries.

FRENCH: Usually considered one of the most romantic languages, French can also be useful in business, especially in the European market. Spoken in over 40 countries, it is also the second most common language found on the Internet, behind English.

JAPANESE: Also known as a very difficult language to learn. It is handy to know, especially if you are considering a career in robotics or foreign relations.

ARABIC: If you are considering a career in the petroleum or defense industry, you may want to look into learning Arabic. Over 300 million people speak this language and it will definitely help your resume stand out.

But, really, any second language you learn will look impressive to potential employers. So if there's a country or language you have always been fascinated by, go for it! Plus, most colleges require a few foreign language credits anyway, so you may as well take classes in something you are really interested in. Some other fun languages to consider:

- Italian

- German

- Welsh

- Latin

Programs like Rosetta Stone and online language courses can be very helpful in getting to know a language, but nothing beats studying in class with a qualified instructor. For even more practice, consider getting a group together from your class and, if possible, with native speakers on campus. Get together once a week and only speak that language. The more you force yourself to formulate sentences out loud, the easier it will come to you.

Nothing helps you learn a language better than total immersion, so why not consider studying abroad in the country where your language is spoken? Imagine being able to flirt with someone in a foreign country in their native tongue!

79

JOIN A CLUB

Just like in high school, extra-curricular activities are extremely important in making yourself a well-rounded individual. In college, the number of clubs you can join is endless. No matter your top interests, there will be a club for that.

The difference between high school clubs and college clubs is that here, you get to pick which ones to join. No more listening to mom and dad about what will look best on that college application. Cause here you are, in college!

There are two reasons to join a club:

1. **IT WILL LOOK DAMN GOOD ON YOUR RESUME.** The clubs here will be tied to your major. Studying engineering? Join the engineering club. Studying journalism? Join the student journalists club. Studying theater? Join the drama club. These clubs will help you make connections with real-world professionals already in your field of work, which could lead to future internship and job opportunities for you.

2. **BECAUSE YOU ARE INSANELY PASSIONATE ABOUT ITS MISSION.** If you want to save the dolphins, then by all means, join the "Save the Dolphins" club. If you want to fight for women's rights, join the feminist club. You'll get to meet like-minded people who are passionate about making a difference. When you really believe in something, you won't hesitate to do the hard work it requires.

To get more out of each club experience, you may also consider taking on a leadership position. In doing so, you'll learn about budgets, event planning, problem-solving, how to effectively communicate, and so much more.

By gaining these experiences, you'll make yourself a better candidate for future jobs. Employers want to see that their employees are well-rounded, can wear a lot of hats, and are efficient multitaskers. All of those skills can be learned and perfected during your time in school clubs.

80

START A NEW CLUB

We've just covered why you should join on-campus clubs, but what if there isn't a club for your special interest? Well, we've got an easy solution for you: form a club of your very own!

It doesn't matter how obscure your interests are, we're willing to bet there are other people on campus who share your passion. For instance, if you love playing a certain game, like poker or Dungeons and Dragons, this is a perfect way to find new players and make friends with people with similar interests. Hell, if you love video games but lack people to play with, start a gamer club!

Do you have a hobby that you would love to share with others? This could be anything from knitting to making collages to collecting comic books. A club is the perfect way to find your like-minded cohorts.

What if you are a superfan of a band, book series, or TV show? Start a club for that too; it's more fun to geek out with a group of people any day! Have a weekly viewing party for your favorite show, or a meetup at the movies for the latest comic book adaptation or your favorite actor's film. The type of club you can form is only limited to your imagination.

Here is just a sampling of the quirky clubs at campuses across the country:

1. Happiness Club (Northwestern University)

2. Squirrel Club (University of Michigan)

3. Skydiving Club (Virginia Tech)

4. People Watching Club (University of Minnesota)

5. Wizards & Muggles, a Harry Potter fan club (College of William and Mary)

6. Cheese Club (SUNY Purchase)

7. Humans vs. Zombies (currently at over 600 campuses nationwide)

81

DO A SUMMER INTERNSHIP

College is a time to prepare for your future. These days, it is nearly impossible to get an entry-level job without already having some internships on your resume. Once you pick your major and you decide that that field of study will also be your career, you will want to start looking for internships in that field.

There are two places on campus that can help you with your search. First, talk to your advisor in your major. He/she will likely already know many websites that list internships in your field or specific companies that regularly hire interns. You can also visit your campus career center. The staff there manages full-time job listings as well as internship ads.

To apply for internships, you'll need to write a cover letter and submit your resume (see page 210 for more information on resumes). If you need tips on writing your cover letter, ask your advisor to help. He/she will be happy to look it over and give you tips and suggestions to make it better.

Many internships are rather competitive, so you'll want to do everything you can to stand out from the rest. Many students try to get internships in the summer, when they don't have to balance their course load with the extra work. If you aren't selected for a summer internship, consider taking one on during the spring or fall semesters, when it's less competitive.

For summer internships, you can also think about traveling to another city. It will give you a different experience outside of the bubble where you live. There may be more details to figure out when traveling, such as housing. You can check with the local colleges if they open their dorms to student interns—many actually do!

Though many internships are unpaid, there are some magical unicorn internships that could include stipends or hourly wages. It all depends on the company's procedures. A paid internship does not look better on a resume than an unpaid internship. All internships, paid and unpaid, count for school credit, so make sure to check what paperwork needs to be filled out for it to count.

If you do a great job during your internship, you should ask your supervisor to be a reference. You can ask them to write you a letter that you can use for future internship applications as well as being a reference on your resume. With one internship under your sleeve, you'll be well on your way to your next one and soon enough you'll have your first real job.

82

CREATE A RESUME

As you apply for internships and jobs, you will need a resume. First rule of resumes: don't lie. Other standard guidelines include using correct spelling and grammar; creating it from scratch (don't use a template!); keeping it to one page (unless you are already a CEO, you do not need a resume that goes past one page), and make it easy to read (stick to ½-inch to 1-inch margins and keep the font size between 10 to 12 points).

At the top of the resume, you'll list your name, phone number, email (keep it professional! No honeybunny26@ gmail.com emails allowed), and street address. Double and triple check these for errors.

Next, you'll want to add in your experience. This can come in a number of headings, such as:

• Internships

• Work experience

• Education or coursework

- Volunteer experience

- Leadership activities

- Computer skills (if applicable for specific programs in your field of work)

- Awards and honors

As you finish your resume, you'll also want to create an account on LinkedIn, which is a networking tool to connect to the people and things that matter in your professional world. On your personalized page (which is essentially your online resume), you can list all the same information on your resume and more.

If at any time you feel lost, head to your campus career center for help.

As you build each section of your resume, you'll want to use action words. Here are some suggestions:

COMMUNICATION: Collaborated; Conducted; Drafted; Edited; Influenced; Mediated; Planned; Presented; Proposed; Reported; Researched; Translated; Wrote.

CREATIVE: Adapted; Conceived; Composed; Developed; Established; Illustrated; Imagined; Improved; Originated; Performed; Publicized; Updated; Visualized.

FINANCIAL: Accounted; Allocated; Audited; Balanced; Budgeted; Calculated; Estimated; Forecasted; Formulated; Invested; Projected.

HUMAN RELATIONS: Advised; Assisted; Counseled; Encouraged; Empowered; Helped; Guided; Joined.

LEADERSHIP: Achieved; Assigned; Coached; Contracted; Delegated; Directed; Evaluated; Formed; Founded; Initiated; Implemented; Led; Managed; Negotiated; Recruited; Supervised.

PROBLEM-SOLVING: Adjusted; Analyzed; Anticipated; Discovered; Eliminated; Examined; Executed; Planned; Resolved; Simplified; Solved; Verified.

RESEARCH: Assessed; Compared; Interviewed; Organized; Surveyed; Summarized.

TECHNICAL: Assembled; Built; Coded; Drafted; Engineered; Inspected; Installed; Maintained; Operated; Programmed; Repaired; Tested.

TRAINING: Demonstrated; Evaluated; Instructed; Taught; Tutored; Trained.

83

MAKE THE DEAN'S LIST

Your parents will be so proud when you tell them the news. To land on the dean's list, your GPA will need to be 3.5 or above (typical for most schools, but may vary). To get such stellar grades, you should study regularly, attend and participate in all your classes, review your notes, and take care of yourself.

While it is all too easy to get distracted by the social scene of college, you have to remember that your academics do come first. It's perfectly okay to take a night off from studying to hang out with friends and recharge your batteries. But you also have to know when to say no to movie night because you have a test coming up. FOMO (fear of missing out) is a real thing, and you will face it head on in college. You can't be in two places at once, and sometimes the fun does have to wait. It only takes a few bad choices to drop your A or B down to a C. And a few more after that to bring your grade to an F.

Making the dean's list is a huge honor and it's proof that you are doing well in college. In fact, you can also use your status as a dean's list scholar to help with financial aid and scholarships. Many scholarships and financial aid packages are merit-based, meaning they are awarded based on individual achievements, such as academic, athletic, or artistic accomplishments. So the better your grades, the better your chances to get scholarships to help with your academic costs.

If you make the dean's list for more than one semester, you will also be recognized at graduation for your achievements. Sometimes, it will include an additional ribbon or sash to wear with your cap and gown.

84

GET A SCHOLARSHIP

Any little chunk of money helps! Do you know how expensive books are?! Well, if you haven't had the chance to buy your books for the semester yet, be prepared. At some point, you will have a book that costs $100. And when you try to sell it back at the end of the semester, you'll only get $10 or $20. No joke. It's a total rip off.

So, scholarships! They can help with those exorbitant costs, including tuition, books, and even on-campus housing.

Scholarships fall into two categories: merit-based scholarships and need-based scholarships. Merit-based scholarships are based on your personal achievements, including academic, athletic, or artistic accomplishments. Need-based scholarships are based on your family's income or your personal income. To calculate what your parents (or you) are expected to contribute to the cost of college, you'll want to fill out the Free Application for Federal Student Aid (FAFSA). After your application is completed, you'll be offered a variety of different financial aid packages, such as work-study, grants, loans, etc., to help close the gap between what your parents can pay and what the total costs of attendance actually are.

Beyond that, you can research scholarships based on a number of factors. You can look for scholarships by your major, by state, and by school. You can look for scholarships based on your athletic achievements, your academic achievements, or even your personal background (minority scholarships). There might even be scholarships offered through your parents' place of employment. If you do the work, you will find free money with your name on it!

85

SET THE CURVE ON A TEST

Your classmates may come to hate you, but trust us, you'll feel like a badass. The best ways to study are for a little bit each night leading up to the test. It's proven to be a better method for retaining information than an all-nighter cram session (though if you have to do that, see page 181 for tips on how to make it a success).

If you are regularly studying the material you are learning, you will feel more prepared for your tests and exams. And you will likely earn better grades.

It is a damn good feeling to finish a test knowing you crushed it. It is a real shitty feeling to finish a test knowing you bombed. So let's agree to make the first feeling happen more often.

That said, it is a wee bit awkward when a classmate tells you they thought that test was impossible when you know it was pretty easy because you knew the material. Just play along and say that you aren't too sure how you did either.

You really don't want to make your friend feel worse than they already do. You can afford to be humble for a minute.

But when a test truly is hard and doesn't touch on any of the material you were told to study, it's great to commiserate with your classmates over a pitcher of beer.

When it comes to the day that you get the tests back and your teacher gives a stern lecture about the lack of preparation for the test except for one student, you know they'll be talking about you. You will have set the curve! If you didn't get a perfect score on the test, but you did do the best in the class, you may have also added a couple extra points on your classmates' exams to fit the new grading scale. And if you did get 100 percent, mad props! Keep crushin' it!

THINGS TO DO WITH FRIENDS THAT YOU'LL NEVER FORGET

Do any of the things on this list on any particular night and we promise you'll have an epic evening with your friends. These will be the nights that go down in history and that you'll talk about for years to come. In 10 years, you'll have a conversation like this:

1: "Remember that night at the Saloon?"

2: "Oh yeah, when Taylor did that thing?"

1: "Yes, that shit was hilarious! Good times, dude."

Karaoke is always a smart idea. In most towns, you can find karaoke nearly any night of the week. Organizing a group Halloween costume will be a perfect photo op! And planning a class prank is something you can laugh about for the rest of your life. Any future kids of yours will get a kick out of those stories too.

After all, college is not meant for having FOMO. It's all about doing shit because YOLO.

86

HOST A DINNER PARTY FOR YOUR FRIENDS AND ROOMMATES

In Learn to Cook on page 135, we discuss the importance of learning to cook some simple meals in order to not have to rely on take-out or the cafeteria. Well, it's time to take it to the next level. Nothing makes you more confident as a cook than feeding other people and having them give you rave reviews. That's right, time to host a grown-ass dinner party!

Maybe the prospect sounds too intimidating to you. Even if your meal goes down in flames, it will still be a learning experience and make for a funny story.

Q: What should I make?

A: This is limited only by your imagination (and skillset). Start with something simple, like a taco bar or a casserole and salad. If you think you can handle it, then by all means try something more complicated. Oh, and don't forget dessert.

Q: What do I do to get ready?

A: First, clean all the common areas where guests will be mingling (kitchen, living room, bathroom). It doesn't have to be spotless, but the night should feel more special than grabbing pizza with your roomies. Clear away the clutter and give the bathroom a once-over. Make sure there's plenty of TP. Create some atmosphere with candles or a string of lights.

For recipe ideas, scroll through Pinterest or Food Gawker and save recipes that look tasty. For your first time hosting a dinner, it's probably best to stick with a dish that either you're already familiar with or that doesn't seem too time consuming. You don't want to spend all your time in the kitchen frantically stirring and chopping; time it so the bulk of the main food is cooked before guests arrive. Don't be afraid to delegate tasks: have a friend or roommate get people drinks when they arrive and introduce people to get the conversation going. Let guests bring a bottle of something or a dessert if they ask. Your guests will enjoy themselves more if you are relaxed and having a good time rather than stressed out. No matter how tasty the food actually comes out they will be thrilled to eat a home-cooked meal for once and not cafeteria food or cold pizza. Bonus: maybe you'll start a tradition and your friends will want to take turns hosting dinner parties!

87

SING KARAOKE OR
PLAY IN A BAND

Almost everyone has had the fantasy of belting out a tune to an admiring crowd. Why not take a chance and give it a shot? It is college, after all, the perfect time to try something new and possibly out of your comfort zone.

The easiest way to make your *American Idol* fantasies come true is, of course, karaoke. This can be a less stressful option because even those who can't carry a tune in a bucket can have the whole crowd singing along and cheering, with the right song choice and the right amount of bravado. Pick a funny, instantly recognizable song and you will have the whole bar on your side in no time. Or, pick one of those "anthem" songs that people seem to be weirdly attached to and scream along to every word (Case in point: "Don't Stop Believin'" by Journey. People go nuts for that song, no matter the crowd.). Or, if you pick a song that was popular for your age group in high school, you will produce instant nostalgia-feels across the whole room.

Okay, so you actually have a decent voice and want to try singing in a more professional capacity. The best way to get yourself out there is at an open mic night. Your college is almost guaranteed to host one, as are local coffee houses and certain bars. Get there early and sign up, and make your voice heard.

Most college towns are chock full of bands who are looking for singers; check bulletin boards, music shops, and online through Craigslist and other places. You never know what band is missing their crucial element to bring it all together: you. Hey, who knows? You guys could end up making it big. And all it took was taking a chance and putting yourself out there.

MARATHON A TV SHOW YOU'VE NEVER SEEN

There are probably a few TV shows you've heard about but never got around to seeing in their heyday. Or maybe there's a new season of a show coming out and you want to get on the fandom bandwagon and play catch-up with what you missed. Perhaps your roommate won't stop talking about how amazing a certain show is. Time for a good, old-fashioned TV marathon!

This is particularly fun when you've been studying and working your ass off all week and just want to turn your brain off and disappear into another world for a while. It's also a great bonding activity to do with your friends/ roommates, especially if you decide to marathon the show that they won't shut up about. (Just try not to strangle them if they keep saying things like "Wait 'til you see when...aghh I can't tell you!")

Thanks to technology, it's now easier than ever to marathon shows of any kind. Netflix, Hulu, Amazon Prime, and

YouTube are just some of the ways you can take a deep dive into the world of a TV show and not emerge for hours (except for snack/bathroom breaks of course!).

Not sure where to start? Here are some genres for you to explore:

SCI-FI AND FANTASY

- *Battlestar Galactica*
- *Buffy the Vampire Slayer*
- *Doctor Who*
- *Farscape*
- *Firefly*
- *Game of Thrones*
- *Lost*
- *Orphan Black*
- *Star Trek*
- *Torchwood*
- *True Blood*
- *Twilight Zone*
- *The X-Files*

DRAMA AND ACTION

- *Breaking Bad*
- *Friday Night Lights*
- *Grey's Anatomy*
- *Mad Men*
- *My So-Called Life*
- *Orange Is the New Black*
- *Queer as Folk*
- *Sherlock*
- *Sons of Anarchy*
- *The Sopranos*
- *Veronica Mars*
- *The West Wing*
- *The Wire*

COMEDY

- *30 Rock*
- *Arrested Development*
- *Broad City*
- *Community*
- *Friends*
- *How I Met Your Mother*
- *Louie*

- *Modern Family*

- *The Office*

- *Parks and Recreation*

- *Sex and the City*

- *Scrubs*

- *Seinfeld*

- *The Simpsons*

- *Veep*

So what are you waiting for? Put the homework aside, put on some comfy lounging clothes, grab some snacks, and dive in!

89

ORGANIZE A GROUP HALLOWEEN COSTUME

Halloween is a milestone for every college student. Gone are the days of trick-or-treating, or sneaking out of your parent's house to try to find a cool party and someone to buy you beer. No, you're a grown-up now, free to dress up in whatever wacky/slutty getup you want to, and hit up as many sloppy house parties or bars that you want!

You know what would make this night even more fun? A group Halloween costume! Not only is it a unique way to bond with your friends and roommates, but if done right, you are guaranteed to get a load of attention wherever you go. A clever and well-planned group costume will have random people begging to take photos of you all night; plus, you are a lock to win any costume contest that you come across.

First things first: What should your idea be? It should be clever, topical, and recognizable to most people. Some categories to get you started:

- TV shows/movies
- Inanimate objects (pack of cards, six pack, dominoes, etc.)
- Pop culture/news stories
- Singers/bands
- Political figures
- Book characters
- Clever puns

Once you've picked your group idea, it's time to get to work. Thrift stores and online shopping sites like Amazon are the best way to get your costume together cheaply. If one of your friends knows how to sew, even better. Look to see if your student discount will work at any craft supplies stores in town as well. Once your costumes are assembled, get ready to have a night you'll never forget! Take lots of pictures!

90

SPEND THANKSGIVING (OR ANY HOLIDAY) WITH YOUR FRIENDS

One rite of passage that every adult experiences is the first holiday away from the family. Maybe you can't afford to go home over break, or you have a lot of studying to catch up on and can't get away. For whatever reason, being away from your family this holiday is no reason for you not to celebrate. In fact, it's a great opportunity to experience one of the joys of being a grown-up: the friend holiday!

Having a holiday with just your friends combines all the fun of the holidays without the added pressure of having to answer a million questions about your life from your relatives, and making sure you don't get too drunk in front of them. With a friend holiday, you all can relax, enjoy the break from school, and maybe even start a new holiday tradition. If it's Thanksgiving or any other holiday that revolves around a big dinner, turn it into a potluck and have everyone contribute something. Or, go completely nontraditional and order pizza or Chinese (be aware: your options may be limited due to it being a holiday and all).

Spending Easter with your pals? Why not have an old-fashioned Easter egg hunt! (The eggs can be cans of beer and other more adult-like treats.) What about the holiday that was made to be celebrated with friends, New Year's Eve? Instead of fighting the crowds at the bars and paying the jacked-up cover charges, why not host a NYE party? Make it a fancy cocktail dress-up affair, or something more casual and spontaneous. Have everyone share at least one resolution for the new year; you could even make a party game out of it. Don't forget to scope out someone to kiss at midnight!

Whatever the holiday, spending one with your friends is sure to make your college experience even more memorable and can cement friendships that last way past college.

91

HAVE A BBQ

If the weather is hot and everyone is jonesing for some quality outdoor time, but there's not enough left of the weekend to head out of town, why not have a BBQ? It's an easy, cheap way to get the whole gang together and soak up the sun while chowing on good grub and drinks.

Where to have a BBQ? Well, the obvious choice is whoever has a yard and owns an outdoor grill. Or whoever lives in an apartment complex with a grilling/picnic area. If everyone you know lives in the dorms, time to head to a local park. Most have permanent grills that anyone can use.

Once you figure out the location, the next crucial element is the food. Any meat products that aren't too much of a hassle and can feed a crowd cheaply are a good plan. Hot dogs, burger patties, and the like. Even chicken can be bought on sale and basted with some good BBQ sauce and you'll be all set. Have vegetarians in the crowd? Grill up some portobello mushrooms or veggie kabobs. Or they can fill up on the side dishes. Side dish ideas can be anything from chips, corn on the cob, beans, potato or macaroni salad, fruit, etc.

This is sounding kind of expensive, you might be thinking. Well the key to keeping costs down is to make it a potluck! Assign each friend with a different element of the cookout (sides, booze, utensils, meat, etc.) so one person isn't left having to shell out major bucks so their friends can fill up.

It's recommended that you follow the advice about day drinking on page 141. Basically, watch your booze intake when you're going to be in the hot sun for hours and drink lots of water.

Oh, and don't forget to bring some fun activities for everyone. Get an impromptu football game going, or even play a childhood game like freeze tag or hide and go seek. With booze!

92

PLAN A CLASS PRANK

College pranks are practically as old as colleges themselves. For whatever reason, having a large population of young adults with plenty of free time and away from home for the first time has always been a recipe for pranking hijinks. It falls to you and your peers to continue in this glorious tradition!

First of all, there are the smaller pranks you can pull on one or more of your friends. Then there are the big guns, where a large segment of the student population bands together to prank the campus and/or the people in charge. You probably should start small in your pranking endeavors and work your way up, culminating in an epic senior prank for the ages!

Easy pranks on your room/dorm mates can include:

• Fill their room with popcorn.

• Saran-Wrap the door.

• Change their phone's ringtones.

• Steal their clothes/towel while they're in the shower.

Be sure to know your pranking victim and make sure they can take a joke. You don't want to end up with an angry roommate who's going to go ballistic on your shit. Conversely, be prepared for the inevitable prank war that may ensue when you prank your pals. Watch your back!

Ready to take your pranking to the next level? Time to spread the mischief campus-wide!

Some ideas include:

• Organize a fake protest.

• Flash mob somewhere on campus.

• Have an entire classroom burst into song during a test.

• Dump soap into the water fountain, and watch the suds fly!

NOTABLE PRANKS

1. In 1958, students at Cambridge University placed a car on the roof of one of the buildings. It took a week for officials to figure out how to get it down.

2. Texas A&M University saw the installation of a giant, 40-foot wide bra on the roof of one of their buildings in 1973.

3. In 2009, University of North Carolina students relieved some finals week stress by organizing a 3,000-person flash mob rave in the library.

Good luck and prank on!

93

MAKE A RIDICULOUS BET WITH FRIENDS

Nothing can make more crazy memories and evoke gales of laughter from your friends than a ludicrous bet. And college is just the place to do something wild and put your money/dignity/stuff on the line for the sake of fun.

What should you bet about? The possibilities are endless! You could go the straightforward sports betting route and put something on the line for whoever's team loses. Winner gets lunch paid for a whole week; loser has to shave their head. Talk about giving that game an extra sense of urgency!

You could also bet your friends to do feats of daring, like wagering an amount of money that they won't eat a disgusting concoction or wear shorts for a month during the winter. Use your imagination and test your mettle!

You may be asking yourself, "Why the hell would I make a crazy bet in the first place? What's the point? And what if I lose?" Well there's a reason this book isn't called *The College*

Only Do Safe Things That Make Sense List. You want to add some hilarious stories to your college experience, right? Then this is one bucket list item you can't pass up!

94

SENIOR YEAR: REVISIT YOUR FRESHMAN PAST

Ahh, senior year: you've overcome your initial insecurities, hopefully have done some kick-ass work in your studies, made some friends, and had some crazy and new experiences (hopefully some from this book!). What better way to reflect on how far you've come than revisiting your freshman past?

First up: have a reunion with your freshman roommates. Maybe you stayed in touch with them and they have remained your close friends throughout college. But there's probably one or two that you may have lost touch with along the way. Why not invite everyone for a dinner to reminisce about your freshman experiences? You will have a blast recounting how nervous you all were, the silly mistakes you might have made, and how much you all have grown. Vow to stay in touch as you all part ways after graduation.

If you feel like imparting some wisdom to the younger generation, why not take a stroll over to your freshman dorm? Check out who's living there now and tell them your experiences and the tips and tricks you learned for making college life easier. If you're feeling generous you could even buy them beer, since they are still underage. Tell them all the things you wished people had told you about.

Is there a professor from one of your freshman classes that was particularly helpful or inspiring? Pay them a visit and thank them for being such a cool instructor for your first year. You will make their day, guaranteed!

What's next? Any damn thing you want. The world is your oyster!

95

FIND OUT WHAT YOUR STUDENT DISCOUNT WILL GET YOU

Unless you are one of the few students with a trust fund to their name (lucky you!), most students are rather poor during their college years. Think lots of ramen noodles, cheap beer, and limited access to entertainment. Being broke can make things stressful (especially when you have to buy a $200 book!), but it's also a learning experience in how to budget as well as how to get creative in stretching each and every dollar you earn.

Many local businesses around your college town will likely offer student deals (coffee houses, nearby delis, even bars near campus), so research those with your friends. See who can find the best student deal. Or ask your student newspaper to compile all the local discounts available to students. As for a more national level, we've provided a list of businesses that are eager to help you students save a couple bucks. Please note, deals may vary on location.

SCHOOL SUPPLIES

FEDEX OFFICE: Save 20 to 30 percent on shipping and printing services.

AMAZON: Prime Student is free for six months, then available with a 50 percent discount.

NEWSPAPERS

THE NEW YORK TIMES: Get student access for $1 a week.

THE WALL STREET JOURNAL: The student offer is $15 for 15 weeks.

CLOTHING AND MERCHANDISE

SAM'S CLUB: Sign up for a collegiate membership with your student ID and a .edu email address.

J. CREW: 15 percent discount in stores and online with a valid student ID.

TOPSHOP: Sign up for the Student Beans iD to save 10 percent in stores and online.

TOMS: Sign up for the Student Beans iD to get notifications of student discounts.

BANANA REPUBLIC: Save 15 percent on full-priced purchases with a valid student ID.

ASOS: Students that register with ASOS get 10 percent off everything.

MADEWELL: 15 percent off in stores with a valid student ID at checkout.

ELECTRONICS AND DIGITAL SERVICES

APPLE STORE: Educational pricing includes deals such as up to $200 off a new Mac.

ADOBE: Purchase student edition software for discounted prices.

NORTON: Up to 50 percent off Norton protection software for your PC, Mac, and more.

HP: Create an HP Student Store account with a .edu email address to access various discounts.

AT&T: Validate your .edu email address to get discounts on cell phones and services.

LOGITECH: Save up to 20 percent on your purchases when you join Logitech Academy.

DELL: Education savings and special packages vary.

SONY: Students receive special pricing on software.

FOOD AND RESTAURANTS

HARD ROCK CAFE: Exclusive discounted menu for students.

SUBWAY: 10 percent off your total purchase (participating locations only).

BURGER KING: Sign up for the Student Beans iD to get notifications of student discounts.

CHICK-FIL-A: At participating locations, students can get a free drink with purchase with a valid student ID.

DAIRY QUEEN: Special student meal deals at participating locations.

SERVICES

STATE FARM INSURANCE: Good Student discount (up to 25 percent off if you get good grades).

ZIPCAR: Discounted membership rates to students.

ESURANCE: Save money when your grades are a B average or better.

JIFFY LUBE: Save $10 or 10 percent with your student ID.

NATIONWIDE INSURANCE: Good Student discount (drivers 16 to 24, with a B average or better).

24-HOUR FITNESS: Special pricing when you sign up.

TRAVELERS INSURANCE: Good Student discount (B average or better).

ALLSTATE INSURANCE: Save up to 25 percent with good grades until you're 26.

GEICO: Students can save up to $200 with the Good Student discount.

TRAVEL

LONELY PLANET: Sign up for an International Student ID Card to save 30 percent off Lonely Planet guides and PDF ebooks.

GREYHOUND: Save 20 percent on fares when you get a Student Advantage Discount Card.

AMTRAK: Save 15 percent on fares when you get a Student Advantage Discount Card.

PUBLIC TRANSPORTATION: Check with local transit authorities for discounted fares.

STA TRAVEL: Special pricing for students.

ENTERTAINMENT

MADAME TUSSAUDS: Student admission packages available.

AMC THEATRES: Admission discounts on Thursdays.

CINEMARK THEATRES: Admission discounts with a valid student ID.

REGAL CINEMAS: Admission discounts vary at locations.

NATIONAL SPORTING EVENTS: Check with your local teams for special student event nights, often including discounted concessions.

96

GO TO A FILM FESTIVAL

Film Festivals are held all over in many different cities. If your city doesn't have its own, there is likely to be one not too far away. You can attend as a guest by buying tickets beforehand. Or you can look into volunteering, in which case, you may get to attend some screenings for free. Here are a few film festivals worth checking out:

100 WORDS FILM FESTIVAL (Charlotte, NC): This annual festival celebrates concise storytelling, as each film must contain exactly 100 spoken words. Held in November.

BIG BEAR LAKE INTERNATIONAL FILM FESTIVAL (Big Bear Lake, CA): This festival is focused on emerging talents in independent filmmaking and screenwriting. Held in September.

BOSTON FILM FESTIVAL (Boston, MA): This festival showcases feature films, documentaries, and shorts. Held in September.

CHICAGO INTERNATIONAL FILM FESTIVAL (Chicago, IL): This festival presents films in contexts that encourage discussion and debate. Held in October.

DANCES WITH FILMS (Los Angeles, CA): This festival celebrates the unknowns, as celebrities are not allowed. Held in June.

GARDEN STATE FILM FESTIVAL (Atlantic City, NJ): This festival promotes the art of filmmaking on all levels and through a variety of film, video, and animated works. Held in March.

LOS ANGELES FILM FESTIVAL (Los Angeles, CA): This festival showcases independent, feature, documentary, and short films, as well as music videos. Held in June.

LOVE YOUR SHORTS FILM FESTIVAL (Sanford, FL): This festival screens only shorts under 30 minutes. Held around Valentine's Day.

SEATTLE INTERNATIONAL FILM FESTIVAL (Seattle, WA): This festival is one of the largest and lasts 25 days. It features films, documentaries, and shorts. Held in May.

SUNDANCE FILM FESTIVAL (Park City, UT): This festival is the largest independent film festival in the US. Held in January.

TRAVERSE CITY FILM FESTIVAL (Traverse City, MI): This festival was cofounded by filmmaker Michael Moore and features independent, foreign, and documentary films. Held in July.

TRIBECA FILM FESTIVAL (New York City, NY): This festival was founded by Jane Rosenthal and Robert De Niro. Held in April.

97

GET A PSYCHIC READING

For as little as $10, you can get a glimpse at your entire future. Grab some friends and head to the local psychic for a palm reading or tarot card reading. Be prepared with some questions. Pick any from the list below.

GENERAL OPEN-ENDED QUESTIONS

(You don't want to ask anything that is particularly leading in any way.)

• I want to know about my future in general.

• Can you see any major changes in my life? In what way?

• What can you tell me about my love life?

• Do you see anything about my health?

• What can you tell me about my career?

QUESTIONS ABOUT LOVE

- What should I do before I start looking for a new relationship?

- How can I prepare myself for a new and healthy relationship?

- To avoid repeating the same mistakes, what do I need to work on with myself?

- What kind of person is most compatible with me?

- What affirmations can I use to attract my soul mate?

WORK AND CAREER

- Why am I so tense at work? What can I do to release this tension?

- How can I succeed in my present job?

- What types of jobs are most suitable for me?

- What job is perfect for me?

- What affirmations would be great for me to allow more money/ get a new job?

98

SPEND TIME ON A LAKE OR RIVER

For those three-day weekends, you've gotta head to some water. Whether it's a lake or river that is closest to campus, you need to grab your swimsuit and your pals and make a long weekend of it.

Do some research to see if there are any campgrounds nearby. If so, then follow our camping tips on page 30. If you plan to make a day trip out of it, that will be splashes of fun as well.

Heading to a lake? Ask around if anyone has access to a boat. Or you can look into daily boat rentals. If you are stuck on land, head to the lake's sandy beach. If you are drinking, be careful with swimming and make sure to keep an eye on all your friends.

Other friends might be more interested in fishing, which can be a fun way to spend the day. Make it a competition to see who can catch the most fish. Make sure to follow local fishing laws.

Spending the day on the river? Get tubes and go floating! You can rent an extra tube to hold a cooler of beer. You'll feel quite relaxed being one with the water and one with your beer. Connect everyone's tube together with rope or by resting your feet on someone else's tube. Be careful not to get separated, as it can take a bit of effort to reconnect with your group if the tide is strong.

Looking for something with a little more thrill? See if your friends want to go white-water rafting.

Make sure someone in your group acts as the photographer for the day. These are photos and memories you'll want to keep!

99

VISIT FRIENDS AT OTHER COLLEGES

Where you go to college is a personal choice. Only you know which school is right for you. And what's right for you might not be what's best for your high school friends. You could very easily be the only person from your high school that is going to your college. Or there could be more than a dozen of you enrolled at the same school. Either way, you are bound to have friends at other colleges across the state and even across the country. Which means, road trip! (See page 27.)

Whenever your schedule allows for it, plan for a weekend away to visit your besties at their universities. You'll get to see a whole new college experience and see how your friend has changed in the time you've been apart. You'll get to meet their new friends and see where they go for fun. And, of course, they'll make the trip to visit you as well.

Be prepared, the reunion might be an emotional one. This is the first time you will see you and your friends moving in separate directions. It won't be easy. Sometimes you may feel forgotten or left behind. Your friend has a whole life that doesn't include you. But you have to remember, you have a new life that doesn't include them either. It will take time and effort from both of you to maintain your friendship. And if your friendship is that important to the both of you, you will be able to manage it.

As you grow up and graduate from college, you and your friends will again be moving in different directions. Some may move for jobs, some may go back to your hometown. Everyone's path is different and you'll be in different places at different times. You must remember not to compare yourself to them. It will be hard, but you can do it.

The lesson is to enjoy all the adventures you have together now. Life is short, and you need to enjoy the moment for as long as it lasts.

100

ATTEND A MUSIC FESTIVAL

Forget Coachella. There are literally hundreds of music festivals around the country every year that have better bands and artists, cooler locales, and fewer annoying celebrities. Like, seriously, leave the Indio desert behind and add one of these festivals to your social calendar. And if you feel like multitasking, pick a festival that requires a road trip with your friends!

GOVERNORS BALL MUSIC FESTIVAL

A three-day festival for people who love all genres of music and all flavors of cuisine.

LOCATION: New York City, NY

TYPICAL MONTH: June

FORMER PERFORMERS: Beck, Bloc Party, Courtney Barnett, Haim, Cold War Kids, Kanye West, The Killers, The Strokes, Jack White, Vampire Weekend, Skrillex, Guns N' Roses, etc.

TICKETS: $275

CAMPING: No

For more info, visit governorsballmusicfestival.com.

BONNAROO MUSIC FESTIVAL

This four-day music festival also offers a comedy stage.

LOCATION: Manchester, TN

TYPICAL MONTH: June

FORMER PERFORMERS: Pearl Jam, Ellie Goulding, Death Cab for Cutie, Judd Apatow and Friends, Tyler the Creator, Elton John, Phoenix, The Flaming Lips, Ice Cube, Cake, etc.

TICKETS: $325

CAMPING: Yes

For more info, visit bonnaroo.com.

FIREFLY MUSIC FESTIVAL

A blend of headlines and emerging artists set among lush wooded landscapes.

LOCATION: Dover, DE

TYPICAL MONTH: June

FORMER PERFORMERS: Ellie Goulding, Ludacris, Flogging Molly, A$AP Rocky, St. Lucia, Blink-182, The 1975, Earth Wind & Fire, Paul McCartney, Kings of Leon, Snoop Dogg, etc.

TICKETS: $129 and up

CAMPING: Yes

For more info, visit fireflyfestival.com.

TELLURIDE BLUEGRASS FESTIVAL

Join the greatest musicians in breathtaking Colorado settings.

LOCATION: Telluride, CO

TYPICAL MONTH: June

FORMER PERFORMERS: Ryan Adams, EmmyLou Harris, Neil Finn, Sam Bush Band, Kacey Musgraves, Janelle Monáe, Ray LaMontagne, Steve Winwood, John Fogerty, etc.

TICKETS: $230 for a four-day pass or $80 per day

CAMPING: Yes

For more info, visit bluegrass.com/telluride.

PITCHFORK FESTIVAL

Promoting the Chicago arts community, this festival also boasts 50 individual vendors and specialty fairs.

LOCATION: Chicago, IL

TYPICAL MONTH: July

FORMER PERFORMERS: Carly Rae Jepsen, Sufjan Stevens, FKA Twigs, Wilco, Sleater-Kinney, James Blake, MIA, Bjork, Yo La Tengo, etc.

TICKETS: $65 per day

CAMPING: No

For more info, visit pitchforkmusicfestival.com.

OUTSIDE LANDS

All major music genres are celebrated alongside food vendors and visual artists to showcase San Francisco's cultural community.

LOCATION: San Francisco, CA

TYPICAL MONTH: August

FORMER PERFORMERS: Radiohead, Lionel Richie, Lana Del Ray, Grimes, Duran Duran, Zedd, Ryan Adams and The Shining, Miguel, etc.

TICKETS: $145 to $355

CAMPING: No

For more info, visit sfoutsidelands.com.

BUMBERSHOOT

A Seattle institution, this festival gathers people from across the country for live music, comedy, theater, film, visual arts, dance performances, and more.

LOCATION: Seattle, WA

TYPICAL MONTH: September

FORMER PERFORMERS: Billy Idol, Fetty Wap, Tyler the Creator, JoJo, Macklemore & Ryan Lewis, Third Eye Blind, Kanye West, A Tribe Called Quest, Blondie, etc.

TICKETS: $180

CAMPING: No

For more info, visit bumbershoot.com.

BOTTLEROCK

Calls itself the best of music, wine, food, and beer.

LOCATION: Napa Valley, CA

TYPICAL MONTH: May

FORMER PERFORMERS: Stevie Wonder, Red Hot Chili Peppers, Lenny Kravitz, Death Cab for Cutie, Michael Franti & Spearhead, Andy Grammer, The Cure, OutKast, Zac Brown Band, etc.

TICKETS: $250

CAMPING: No

For more info, visit bottlerocknapavalley.com.

|Ø|

SPEND AN ENTIRE DAY WATCHING MOVIES WITH YOUR ROOMIES

Put the books down! That's an order. It's time for a mental break with movies! For your own VIP film festival, assign each roommate to a particular task—drinks, popcorn, snacks, films. PJs required, of course. Not sure which movies to screen? Here are some college and coming-of-age movies every undergrad should see!

1. *National Lampoon's Animal House*. If only to understand where toga parties came from.

2. *Good Will Hunting*. Baby Ben Affleck and Matt Damon.

3. *Revenge of the Nerds*. Root for the underdogs!

4. *Old School*. When dudes just can't grow up.

5. *The House Bunny*. Totally underrated and really sweet. Emma Stone before she became Emma Stone.

6. *The Social Network*. If we could become Zuckerberg...

7. *Legally Blonde*. Elle Woods is our homegirl.

8. *Pitch Perfect*. You can't not sing along.

9. *Accepted*. When you take your future into your own hands.

10. *Drumline*. Band geeks? Try band chic!

11. *Mona Lisa Smile*. So many feels about this movie.

12. *Road Trip*. Straight up raunch. Be prepared.

13. *Rudy*. And it's based on a true story!

14. *EuroTrip*. Scotty doesn't know...

15. *Monsters University*. If only we could have applied here instead.

16. *The Devil Wears Prada*. Is that really what the real world is like?

17. *The Graduate*. It's a classic. Discuss it with your parents.

18. *Love & Basketball*. This movie has everything.

19. *The Sisterhood of the Traveling Pants 1 & 2*. Yay friendships.

20. *Frances Ha*. Give it all you've got.

21. *Ruby Sparks*. Bringing magic to real life.

ABOUT THE AUTHORS

Kourtney Jason is a writer, editor, publicist, and pop-culture connoisseur. During her four and a half years of college, she made the dean's list, wrote for her school newspaper, joined clubs, memorized weekly drink specials around town, and maybe did a keg stand or two. In addition to earning her bachelor's degree in news-editorial journalism, Kourtney also earned a degree in how to hold her liquor, thanks to the dozen-plus bars within walking distance of the California State University, Chico campus. Since graduating in 2007, she has moved to NYC twice, authored five books, traveled to Europe three times, and married the love of her life in California and again in Turkey. She writes about celebrities and entertainment for *Metro US*, GossipGirl.com, and YourTango.com as well as hosts a monthly Hollywood gossip segment on At a Glance Talk Radio with Rodney Bardin. She currently lives in Jersey City, New Jersey. Read more of her work at KourtneyJason.com and follow her pop culture musings on Twitter (@kourtneyjason).

Darcy Pedersen is an actress, editor, and comedic writer. She graduated from certified party school California State University, Chico with a degree in theatre arts and has been involved in multiple productions throughout Northern California. She has accomplished a number of items on this bucket list and if you give her the right amount of whiskey, she'll tell you which ones. She currently lives in Northern California.

31901060114032